Digital Poetry

"*Digital Poetry* takes us beyond the frontier of poetic expression in the digital age by questioning its hybrid and multidisciplinary nature and focusing in emerging genres explored in various techno-environments. The field of electronic literature, where Digital Poetry sits, is constantly changing due to the speed of change of digital technologies and this book is a great contribution to this wider field exposing the evolving nature of e-poetry through its most current artistic practices and poetic expressions."

—Dr Maria Mencia, Associate Professor, *Kingston University, London*

Jeneen Naji

Digital Poetry

palgrave
macmillan

Jeneen Naji
Department of Media Studies
National University of Ireland, Maynooth
Maynooth, Ireland

ISBN 978-3-030-65961-5   ISBN 978-3-030-65962-2   (eBook)
https://doi.org/10.1007/978-3-030-65962-2

Cover pattern © Melisa Hasan

This Palgrave Macmillan imprint is published by the registered company Springer Nature
Switzerland AG.
The registered company address is: Gewerbestrasse 11, 6330 Cham, Switzerland

ACKNOWLEDGEMENTS

This book was written during the summer of 2020 during Covid lockdowns, which at the time of submission in September 2020 were still ongoing with no end in sight. Schools and campuses have thankfully reopened but for how long remains to be seen. The impact of school and child care closures hit female academics hard with it being documented by some academic journals, such as the *British Journal for the Philosophy for Science* and *Comparative Political Studies*, that submissions by women had plummeted as Fazackerley outlined in her article *Women's research plummets during lockdown—but articles from men increase* in the *Guardian* online on 12 May 2020. I mention this to celebrate my small cyberspec of achievement that is the writing and submission of this book, a task that in the busy 8 years since I graduated from my PhD seemed impossible and yet was accomplished in the most impossible of times. This is a short book, but one that I believe contributes to the field of digital poetry, and turned out in fact to be my saviour during turbulent times. The solitude and focus of a stolen few hours working on this book early in the morning proved to be one of the best parts of my day and offered me a space of certitude in an increasingly uncertain world. I don't know when lockdowns will end or when a vaccine will be developed, but I do know digital poetry, so it's on that that I have focused. I know we all have our challenges, and many are facing ones much, much, worse than I am during the age of Coronavirus, but I wanted to take a moment to celebrate with you this small miracle that you are reading now. I wrote a book, it is mine and I am so proud of it. Thank you to those who helped, you know who you are, and thank you to my mother who had a voracious intellect and taught me to always respect people's thoughts and ideas. Thank you also to my daughter, who was often content to sit by my side, eat popcorn and watch YouTube kids while I wrote.

CONTENTS

CHAPTER 1

Introduction

Abstract This chapter gives a broad introduction and overview of the hybridic nature of the digital poem and the multidisciplinary field it inhabits. It offers a brief synopsis of each chapter in order to introduce readers to the topics and themes covered in this book on digital poetry such as hermeneutics, posthumanism, communication and interaction. Discussions take place regarding the nature of digital poetry and the impact of the various forms that it takes in relation to human literary expression in a digital age. This chapter highlights the value and topicality of digital poetry research and introduces the broader issues at play in relation to a critical analysis that uses the poetic form and contemporary digital technologies to unpack the dynamics of human subjectivities in cyberspace.

Keywords Digital poetry • Digital humanities • Cyberspace • Code • Technosocialism

In 1986 I was 11 years old and my eldest brother, who had recently secured an Apple Macintosh computer dealership in County Cork, Ireland, brought home a Macintosh Plus computer for Christmas. As the youngest in my family by 15 years, when the excitement of Christmas was over and all had returned to their adult lives elsewhere, the Macintosh and I were left to our own devices in rural Cork countryside. Whilst the dog clearly doubted the machine's potential for fun, I was hooked. I explored the

J. Naji, *Digital Poetry*, https://doi.org/10.1007/978-3-030-65962-2_1

innovative game *Where in the World Is Carmen Sandiego?* (Brøderbund Software 1985) and software such as MacPaint and HyperCard. I began to transcribe poems that I picked out from books onto the computer, eventually composing my own. I stretched and enlarged the font of the poems as far as it would go despite not having the capability to print as we did not yet own a printer. That essentially was how it started, the experience was completely different to loading games from tape on the Commodore 64 computer, which involved hours of staring at the myriad of colours and patterns on screen in the vain hope that this time the game had loaded correctly. Comparative to my previous computing experiences at this stage, the Macintosh was easy to use and most importantly allowed me to use the computer creatively without knowledge of a programming language. This is where it began.

A MULTIDISCIPLINARY APPROACH FOR A COMPLEX ARTEFACT

It is clear that the proliferation of technology and Internet use in today's society has provided a new and varied means for human expression. Digital technologies continue to change and develop at a rapid pace and the use of these technologies to create new literary experiences is something in which we, as both producers and consumers, can and will become more expert. This book meshes existing theories from the fields of media studies, philosophy, literature, computer science and even geography in order to critically analyse poetic transformations from paper to pixel. I mention computer science specifically as this book seeks to identify technologically innovative contemporary digital poetry not only through its textual, visual, aural aspects but also through its technical aspects such as code. Digital poetry is a contemporary genre that spans many disciplines and methodologies, its nature is mutable, and its products are characteristically hybridic. One constant however is the use of the digital apparatus to both construct and experience its artefacts. This technosocial book will address the critical problematics of digital poetry hermeneutics by drawing together analytical frameworks of interpretation, communication, posthumanism, interaction and multimodality in order to develop a comprehensive complex model for digital poetics.

This book is not so much concerned with media studies' problematics such as the technological versus social determinism debate but more so with humanities concerns such as the impact of the apparatus on poetic expression and human subjectivities in cyberspace. The potential for literary expression is ever defined by the historical and cultural context in which it occurs, which of course includes the technology available for achieving such expression. The tools and technology in this case are digital which would allow for this book to fall squarely in the field of digital humanities. Poetry in particular is the most appropriate selection for a contemporary study such as this because the interpretive freedom inherent in poetry as a result of its mutable signifiers is also present in the digital medium. In both poetry and the digital world, the potentialities of meaning are mutable as the construction of meaning is dependent on the context, background, platform and socio-cultural situation of the human interpreter.[1] Poetic expression has long been considered emblematic of the human condition and as such studying the impact of the apparatus on human poetic expression is significant. It allows us to begin to critically examine and understand the implications of a move to an age in which a "networked cybernetic system is installed as the medium of communication and knowledge" (Dewdney and Ride 2006: 305).

Like most fields of study, female representation in the areas of digital poetry scholarship and practice is a work in progress and as such this book aims to help contribute to the rectification of this. I offer my approach within the context of Garoian and Gaudelius' (2001: 339) framework for a cyborg identity that enables a subject's agency within digital culture by repositioning the subject to critique digital reproduction in order to imagine and produce new images, ideas, identities and utopias based on their personal cultural perspectives and desires. It must also be noted, however, that my choice of examples reflects my own sphere of practice, culture and experience, specifically that of an Iraqi/Irish mixed heritage female academic in a Northern European University and I, like Sarah Sloane (2000: 13), "am a woman trained in rhetorical and literary analysis ... who is living through the transition from late print culture to early silicon culture." The media landscape that digital poetry objects inhabit is a complex technologically mediated one which, according to Frosh 2019: 164), demonstrates performance as mediation as overt, continual activity. When we think of Hayles' suggestion that a digital poem is a performance or process rather than an object we can see that it mirrors quite closely the

---

[1] See Chap. 3, "Instapoetics and the Literary Algorithm," for an explanation and discussion of the term human interpreter.

complex characteristics of digital media poetics as Frosh outlines in his book *Digital Media Poetics*. This is why as a genre digital poetry is crucial to examine as it is at the very intersection of technology, society and communication. As outlined in Chap. 2, "What Is Digital Poetry?", the very first experimentation outside of the usual mathematical problems conducted on one of the very first stored computers was love poetry.

Joanna Zylinska's book *AI Art: Machine Visions and Warped Dreams* (2020) is valuable in its approach in that she recognises that the analysis of the technological aspect of art is an important factor in any analytical framework of AI Art (Zylinska 2020: 15). The art that Zylinska and the art world are concerned with is primarily visual in nature and indeed that is reflected in the majority of AI Art analysis. Whilst poetry is an artform that includes an aspect of visuality, it is text or language that is most usually an important bearer of meaning in the communicative and creative process. Therefore John Cayley's 2018 book *Grammalepsy: Essays on Digital Language Art* is more useful here. John Cayley (2018: 1) believes that language's materiality is singular and as a digital poet or as he terms himself a digital language artist he works with language as if it was his medium. Language, Cayley (2018: 2) observes, only comes into being as a function of reading, language only becomes language within the practice of language (Cayley 2018: 3). As with most theoretically important insights this seems obvious once stated and yet unnoticed until recognised. I see value in the intersection of this approach with the language of machines—code, most code is ineffective unless it is understood within the context of the specific programming language it is written in. A browser will make no sense of your page of perfectly written html code unless you include the opening <HTML> tag at the start of the page. Similarly Cayley (2018: 3) gives the example of gesture remaining just that a gesture until it becomes a sign within the world of practice that is sign language. Cayley's (2018) concept of language as a medium, for digital language art, is intriguing and worth exploiting further in the context of the digital medium and more specifically within the context of code as a medium of language. Again to bring this into the realm of digital language art what then do we make of the semiotic content of interactive gesture within the world of virtual reality (VR) and haptic mobile devices? This question is discussed in Chap. 4, "Haptic Hermeneutics and Poetry Apps," and Chap. 6, "Poetic Mirror Worlds and Mixed Reality Poetry," of this book.

Examples of digital poetry such as Donnachie and Simionato's (2019) *The Library of Nonhuman Books* illustrate the kind of contemporary technosocial literary artefacts that exist in today's digital age. *The Library of Nonhuman Books* is what Donnachie and Simionato term "a reading-machine," that uses physical books and machine learning to act as a bridge between human and non-human readers (2019: 297). The machine learning algorithm "reads" books from between the mid-fifteenth century and the late twentieth century and then creates new versions which are then projected on the wall along with imagery sourced from online. The human interpreter can read the original print book in the machine's "cradle" while the machine also "reads" the printed book, searches online for accompanying Creative Commons[2] (n.d. Online) imagery which it projects onto the walls along with its own "interpretation" of the original print text. A small library of the machine learning version of the books is also exhibited (Donnachie and Simionato 2019: 298). The outputs of the reading machine can be considered poetic in form and therefore categorised as digital poetry, the authors outline how "the reading machine's default settings searches for a low density syllable-based new reading for deriving semantic meanings, reminiscent of a Haiku poem" (Donnachie and Simionato 2019: 300) and that alternative variations can be activated to interpret the printed word through either semantic synthesis or lexical visualisations such as concrete poetry (Donnachie and Simionato 2019: 300–301). Donnachie and Simionato (2020: Online) explain that, in fact, their reading machine creates an "illuminated book of poetry" by reading and interpreting book pages. The authors ask, "what will poetry become, with an algorithm as our muse?" (Donnachie and Simionato 2020: Online). It is this question that lies at the heart of this book but I suggest phrasing it somewhat differently to ask, *what has poetry become since algorithms learnt to read?* More recent algorithms exhibit far more agency in the literary process than ever before and we must now recognise that in fact with the proliferation of machine learning perhaps it is the human who is the muse of the machine.

Chap. 2, "What Is Digital Poetry?", attempts to define the genre of digital poetry, and although this has been done before and done very well (see Funkhouser 2007; Bootz and Salceda 2014; Mencia 2017; Tabbi 2017; Rettberg 2019), because of the continuously changing landscape of technology, the field now needs updating in light of recent technological developments such as drones, virtual reality and artificial intelligence. Furthermore because of the fact that digital poetry was originally defined

---

[2] Creative commons is an online non-profit network of legally shareable content.

by the software that created it, as software and operating systems become defunct so too do we potentially lose entire genres of digital poetry, that is why research projects such as *Pathfinders* (Grigar and Moulthrop n.d.: Online) are invaluable as they aim to document and preserve pieces of electronic literature. This book however seeks to look forward while building on the past, and Chap. 2 does also give brief mention of the history of the Electronic Literature Organisation (n.d.: Online). As Hayles (2012: 13) tells us, digital texts can no longer be regarded as singular standalone objects rather they are constantly changing assemblages in which inequalities and inefficiencies in their operations drive them towards breakdown, disruption, innovation and change. This chapter draws out the problematics of definition of the highly hybridic object that is a digital poem in order to situate the following chapters within an identifiable framework of practice.

Code or the algorithm is a subject that this book is particularly concerned with, and Chap. 3, "Instapoetics and the Literary Algorithm," specifically examines code through examples of Instapoetry and machine learning algorithms. This book considers a critical code studies approach, as put forth by Marino (2020: 18) who states that critical code studies grew out a desire to read digital objects with more attention to their unique construction. Here then this book seeks to place digital poetry at the intersection of language, art, code, not only incorporating the surface elements of image and text but also the deeper semiotic undercurrents of language, code and meaning only made real by the presence of the human interpreter. This brings us back to Jenny Weight's technosocial argument of a trilogical relationship that consists of three partners, the human programmer or artist, the executing apparatus and the human interpreter (Weight 2006: 414).

The high sales of Instapoets' poetry books online provide evidence that poetry still has the potential to connect with its audience, but it is also equally clear that the advent of the digital has impacted greatly on audiences. In Chap. 4, "Haptic Hermeneutics and Poetry Apps," I examine digital poetry on mobile platforms in order to contribute to theories of digital rhetoric and help develop a theory of interpretation or meaning making for mobile digital poetry. This is done by situating haptic gesture within a hermeneutic framework that can potentially offer the human interpreter an embodied literary experience. The closed nature of mobile app systems is discussed in terms of its impact on accessing and creating digital poetry for mobile platforms.

Chapter 5, "Eco-Writing and Drones: Digital Poetry During the Anthropocene," examines contemporary digital eco-writing and digital methods of resistance that seek to highlight, combat and draw attention to societal and ecological concerns. The ecological implications and repercussions of the widespread use and proliferation of digital technology are an inconvenient truth. This is why Chap. 5 looks at examples of eco-writing and digital ecopoetry and asks, how can digital technologies that are implicated in the very processes they critique be used as methods of resistance? Chapter 5 discusses how technologies such as drones that were originally envisaged for military or commercial use have been quickly subsumed into a new art world of digital artistic practice and poetic expression such as drone poetry.

Chapter 6, "Poetic Mirror Worlds and Mixed Reality Poetry," explores Mixed Reality (MR) which is best understood within the context of a reality-virtuality continuum which spans from the real environment to augmented reality (AR) and virtual reality (VR) (Milgram et al. 1995). Words in virtual space are examined as multimodal artefacts that take on more of the characteristics of sculptures than text in 3D space. VR projects that incorporate considerable use of text are examined in order to ask questions regarding human embodiment and interaction in digital mirror worlds.

Chapter 7, "Conclusion: Future Poetics: Literary Expression in the Second Age of Machines," restates the conclusions formed in previous chapter and situates contemporary digital poetry within the second age of machines. The vastly different poetic implications of the nature of the differing digital poetry techno-environments discussed in each chapter are recapped such as the haptic hermeneutics of mobile platforms and the deifying distance of VR and drone interactions. The future of modern poetic writing was identified as requiring greater consideration of the function of literary algorithms as human interpretative autonomy was diminished in final poetic output but enhanced in initial coding creation. The final chapter outlines how this book has sought to understand how the literary experience is transformed in contemporary computing environments in order to offer a more critical and considered engagement with such systems that may inform and anticipate an understanding of current and future human literary engagement in the virtual space.

SUMMARY

This chapter introduced the digital poetry artefact as a hybridic object that inhabits a dynamic networked landscape of differing techno-environments. The value and topicality of digital poetry research were highlighted and each chapter of this book was introduced in order to set the groundwork for the following chapters. The broad issues of hermeneutics, posthumanism, gesture as meaning making and technosocial multimodal communication were introduced along with their relevance to the critical analysis of digital poetry.

REFERENCES

Bootz, P., and H. Salceda. 2014. *Litterature et Numerique: quand, comment, pourquoi?* Paris: Presses Universitaires du Nouveau Monde.

Brøderbund Software. 1985. Where in the World Is Carmen Sandiego? *Deluxe* Is a Video Game within the Carmen Sandiego.

Cayley, J. 2018. *Grammalepsy.* New York: Bloomsbury.

Creative Commons. n.d. Online. Accessed 17 September 2020. https://creativecommons.org/.

Dewdney, A., and P. Ride. 2006. *The New Media Handbook.* London and New York: Routledge.

Donnachie, K., and A. Simionato. 2019. The Library of Nonhuman Books. In *xCoax2019: Proceedings of the Seventh Conference on Computation, Communication, Aesthetics & X*, 297–301. Milan, Italy.

———. 2020. Friday Essay: A Real Life Experiment Illuminates the Future of Books and Reading. In *The Conversation.* Accessed 17 September 2020. https://theconversation.com/friday-essay-a-real-life-experiment-illuminates-the-future-of-books-and-reading-131832.

Electronic Literature Organisation. n.d. Online. Accessed 7 September 2020. https://eliterature.org/about/120/.

Frosh, P. 2019. *The Poetics of Digital Media.* Medford, MA: Polity.

Funkhouser, C.T. 2007. *Prehistoric Digital Poetry: An Archaeology of Forms, 1959–1995.* Alabama: The University of Alabama Press.

Garoian, C.R., and Y. Gaudelius. 2001. Cyborg Pedagogy: Performing Resistance in the Digital Age. *Studies in Art Education* 42(4): 333–47. Accessed 8 September 2015. jstor.org/stable/1321078.

Grigar, D., and S. Moulthrop. n.d. Online. *Pathfinders.* Accessed 23 September 2020. http://dtc-wsuv.org/wp/pathfinders/.

Hayles, N.K. 2012. *How We Think, Digital Media and Contemporary Technogenesis.* Chicago: University of Chicago Press.

Marino, M. 2020. *Critical Code Studies*. Cambridge, MA: The MIT Press.

Mencia, M., ed. 2017. *#WomenTechLit*. Morgantown: West Virginia University Press.

Milgram, P., H. Takemura, A. Utsumi, and F. Kishino. 1995. Augmented Reality: A Class of Displays on the Reality-Virtuality Continuum. In *Telemanipulator and Telepresence Technologies*, vol. 2351, 282–293. International Society for Optics and Photonics. December.

Rettberg, S. 2019. *Electronic Literature*. Polity: Cambridge.

Sloane, S. 2000. *Digital Fictions: Storytelling in a Material World*. Stamford, CT: Ablex Publishing Corporation.

Tabbi, J. 2017. *Bloomsbury Handbook of Electronic Literature*. London: Bloomsbury.

Weight, J. 2006. I, Apparatus, You: A Technosocial Introduction to Creative Practice. *Convergence: The International Journal of Research into New Media Technologies* 12 (4): 413–446.

Zylinska, Joanna. 2020. *AI Art, Machine Visions and Warped Dreams*. London: Open Humanities Press.

CHAPTER 2

What Is Digital Poetry?

Abstract This chapter will define the genre of digital poetry and its components and also include a brief discussion of the history of digital poetry. As Hayles (*How We Think, Digital Media and Contemporary Technogenesis.* Chicago: University of Chicago Press, 2012: 13) tells us, digital texts can no longer be regarded as singular standalone objects rather they are constantly changing assemblages in which inequalities and inefficiencies in their operations drive them towards breakdown, disruption, innovation and change. The sharing economy of the internet, as it is termed, means that contemporary cultural content such as poetry cannot be separated from the communities and platforms that both form and read them. This chapter draws out the problematics of definition of the hybridic object that is a digital poem in order to situate the following chapters within an identifiable framework of practice.

Keywords Hybridic • Process • Mutable • Poetry • History • Technocentric

A Brief History of Digital Poetry

Digital poetry and digital literature are most usually referred to as electronic literature (Emerson 2014: xiii). In fact, the field of electronic literature has gained momentum and popularity from a niche area of knowledge into an increasingly recognised discipline that can be used to chart the affordances and constraints of the digital medium. Research groups and projects such as *Digital Digital Digital Littérature* (DDDL) in France, *Hermeneia* in Spain, *Electronic Literature as a Model of Creativity and Innovation in Practice* (ELMCIP) in Norway, *Poetry in the Digital Age* in Germany and the *PO.EX* in Portugal are all concerned with research and practice in the area of electronic literature. Also the extremely active American-based international Electronic Literature Organization (ELO) runs annual conferences and publishes digital collections of electronic literature among many other activities in order to foster and promote the reading, writing, teaching and understanding of literature as it develops and persists in a changing digital environment. The contemporary prevalence of digital technologies and online content creation means that the field of electronic literature, and its sub-set digital poetry, is increasingly recognised as entering into mainstream consciousness. As a result, the question as to whether a digital poem can really be considered a poem or even literature is no longer considered seriously. Instead our efforts are steered more usefully towards driving and charting the changing shape of the text in a contemporary digital age and formulating a thoughtful engagement with immersive computing technologies. However, this does not mean that we disregard previous models of criticism, the application of traditional analogue theoretical models is still useful in order to chart the changing shape of cultural expression. In fact, rather than replacing existing and past cultural knowledge and forms, digital tools and techniques can instead draw on and highlight previous literary models, often bringing a renewed interest and an understanding of historical cultural objects. Dene Grigar, president of the Electronic Literature Organisation from 2013–2019, describes electronic literature as a challenging art form that may involve visual, sonic, kinetic and kinaesthetic modalities and possess, to varying degrees, literariness; however, the common denominator of all works of electronic literature is that it is computational (Grigar 2014: Online). The ELO was formed in 1999 and according to its web site one of its goals is to draw attention to "born-digital literature" (ELO n.d.: Online). To date the ELO has published online three collections of electronic literature, and from September 2011 to July 1, 2017, these were housed at MIT's Media Lab after which the ELO and its collections were moved to Washington State University Vancouver (ELO: Online).

Rettberg (2019: 20), one of the founders of the ELO (along with Robert Coover and Jeff Ballowe in 1999), defines combinatory poetics as the oldest genre of electronic literature with Christopher Strachey's *Love Letters* generator in 1952. Stratchey like Turing was gay so *Love Letters* is often discussed within the context of queer identity, and he produced a simple algorithm that drew on around 70 base words which meant that potentially 300 billion love letters could be produced (Roberts 2017: Online). This was a combinatory algorithm for the Manchester Ferranti Mark 1 computer (Wardrip-Fruin 2005: Online) which was the first stored program digital computer and it used a cathode-ray tube (CRT) display for its storage, a methodology most similar to what we use today for computing. A stored program digital computer was a landmark development after Turing's machine because it meant that the computer could store (and potentially modify) its own instructions as well as its data. Its instructions or algorithms were also part of its data, and once all that data is digital, well then it is programmable, and then concurrently it is only natural that someone wants to see what else the machine can do apart from solving complex mathematical problems.

European digital poetic experimentation has historically been wide reaching and fruitful, from the first experiments in digital poetry by the Ouvroir de Litterature Potentielle (OULIPO) group founded in 1960 by French mathematician Francois de Lionnais and writer Raymond Queneau, to E. M. de Melo e Castro's production of video poetry in Portugal during the 1960s and the computer poetry shown in 1975 at Europalia, an international arts festival in Brussels (Funkhouser 2007: xxi–xxiv). In 1989 the Parisian group LAIRE (Lecture, Art, Innovation, Recherche, Écriture) created the web-based literary journal *Alire*. This included Philippe Bootz, Frédéric Develay, Jean-Marie Dutey, Claude Maillard and Tibor Papp; Bootz states that it is the oldest multimedia journal in Europe (Bootz 1999, Online). *Alire* was "the first periodical on disk dedicated to the publication of digital poetry" (Bootz, Online). Bootz believes that historically, "the journal corresponds to the establishment of a 'third stream' in computerized literature, if one acknowledges that hypertext and earlier software texts made up the first two. This third stream being that of animated literature, to which the five authors from LAIRE came from backgrounds in aural and visual poetry Video poetry clearly was an important precursor to the development of screen based digital poetry in aural and visual poetry" (Bootz, Online). The Electronic Poetry Center (EPC) at the University of Buffalo, USA, was founded in 1995. The EPC also provided access to digital poetry works and resources. Their aim was "to make available a wide range of resources centred on digital and contemporary formally innovative poetries, new media writing, and literary programming" (ELO: Online). Loss Pequeño Glazier was the director and founder of the EPC and is a digital poet and academic. His book *Digital Poetics: The Making of E-Poetries* (Glazier 2002) is considered one of the earliest monographs published in the field of digital poetry (Bootz and Baldwin 2010: xiv). Baldwin (Bootz and Baldwin 2010: xiv) suggests Bolter's (2001) *Writing Space* and Hayles' (2008) *Electronic Literature* as landmark texts that have emerged from predominantly American academia. In an effort to counteract the American-centric focus of the published academic work in the field of digital poetry, Bootz and Baldwin edited *Regards Croisés* (2010) a collection of essays on digital literature written by academics from around the globe. However Eduardo Kac had previously attempted a similar venture in 2007 when he edited *Media Poetry, An International Anthology*.

A notable early academic publication exists however in the form of *New Media Poetry: Poetic Innovation and New Technologies* (Kac 1996), an edition of the journal *Visible Language*. It contains articles from international digital poets and academics such as Bootz, Cayley, Melo e Castro, Györi, Kac, Rosenberg, Vallias and Vos. Additionally, other noteworthy publications in the field of electronic literature are Chris Funkhouser's 2007 *Prehistoric Digital Poetry: An Archaeology of Forms, 1959–1995*, Amerika's 2007 *Meta/Data: A Digital Poetics*, Kac's 2007 *Media Poetry, An International Anthology*, Hayles 2008 *Electronic Literature: New Horizons for the Literary*, Bouchardon's 2009 *Littérature numérique: Le récit interactif*, Bootz and Salceda's 2014 *Littérature et Numérique: quand, comment, pourquoi?*, Simanowski's 2011 *Digital Art and Meaning: Reading Kinetic Poetry, Text Machines, Mapping Art, and Interactive Installations*, Strehovec's 2016 *Text as Ride*, Maria Mencia's 2017 *#WomenTechLit*, Joseph Tabbi's 2017 *Bloomsbury Handbook of Electronic Literature*, Scott Rettberg's 2019 *Electronic Literature* book and O'Sullivan's 2019 *Towards a Digital Poetics: Electronic Literature & Literary Games*. However, out of all the book publications mentioned so far, the only ones to focus specifically on digital poetry are Glazier (2002), Kac (1996) and Funkhouser (2007) who offered a very detailed history of the form from 1959 to

1995. I have done my best to list all the scholarly publications that I am aware of in the area of electronic literature and digital poetry, although as human fallibility must prevail, I am sure I will have unintentionally omitted some texts and to those authors I apologise in advance. I list these publications in order to highlight the existence of electronic literature and digital poetry as a field of legitimate scholarly study and to illustrate that the history of digital poetry has been written about extensively and thoroughly so I will not repeat it here. Most accounts of digital poetry seek to place it historically as building on a tradition of concrete poetry. This approach is accurate and beneficial; however, it is linked somewhat to a need to validate digital poetry as poetry, and I wonder how many discussions of traditional poetry require a restating and historical contextualising of each genre within the broader movements of cultural genres. This might have been necessary in the earlier days of the recognition of digital poetry as digital literature, but things have moved on since so that, thanks to the work of those who have gone before, digital poetry is a well-established cultural genre in its own right. Discussions now that are more useful to us are more concerned with the changing shapes of digital poetry and detailed critical analyses of how digital poems function both as poetic objects and contemporary cultural artefacts. This is why this chapter will not provide a detailed history of digital poetry, the brief overview I have outlined above will have to suffice and I direct those readers who hunger for more to the rigorous relevant sources that I have already cited here. The efforts of this book and more specifically this chapter can instead be steered towards asking what digital poetry is.

WHAT IS DIGITAL POETRY?

Of all the literary forms poetry is the most visceral and closely entwined and concerned with the human condition. Literature started as poetry and the poetic form offers a greater flexibility of language and potentiality of meaning than drama and narrative can. It is important to state that this book comes from a place of passion for poetry, a desire to encourage, remember and reinvigorate poetry, not to forget print traditions of the past but instead to use them and draw on them to help build the future. Landow (2006: 13) tells us that when Bush conceptualised the Internet in *The Memex* in his 1945 seminal paper *As We May Think* he created what are essentially poetic machines that is, machines that work "according to analogy and association, machines that capture and create the anarchic brilliance of human imagination. Bush, we perceive, assumed that science and poetry work in essentially the same way" (Landow 2006: 13). It is at this intersection of science and poetry that this research finds itself and it is these poetic machines creating works of analogy and association that are the realisation of our electric dreams.

To understand what digital poetry is, it is first necessary to look at and define electronic literature or digital literature as this is the broad field into which digital poetry falls. Hayles (2008: 3) however posits that electronic literature was generally considered to exclude print literature that has been digitised, that is, it was required to be "born digital." The ELO convened a committee of creators and critics of electronic literature in order to arrive at a suitable definition for the field (Hayles 2008: 3). As part of this definition the ELO states that it is concerned with the investigation of literature produced for the digital medium (ELO: Online). Therefore, the term not only refers to pieces of literature created solely in and experienced through the computer but also those works that began in print before moving to the digital. The ELO (Online) defines electronic literature as *works with important literary aspects that take advantage of the capabilities and contexts provided by the stand-alone or networked computer. Within the broad category of electronic literature are several forms and threads of practice, some of which are:*

- *Hypertext fiction and poetry, on and off the Web*
- *Kinetic poetry presented in Flash and using other platforms*
- *Computer art installations which ask viewers to read them or otherwise have literary aspects*
- *Conversational characters, also known as chatterbots*
- *Interactive fiction*
- *Novels that take the form of emails, SMS messages, or blogs*
- *Poems and stories that are generated by computers, either interactively or based on parameters given at the beginning*
- *Collaborative writing projects that allow readers to contribute to the text of a work*
- *Literary performances online that develop new ways of writing.*
(ELO: Online)

N. Katherine Hayles in her paper *Electronic Literature: What Is It?* (Hayles 2007: Online) observes that electronic literature, while created and performed in the context of networked programmable media, is also informed by the powerhouses of contemporary culture, namely games, films, animations, digital arts, graphic design and electronic visual culture. As such Hayles (2007: Online) refers to it as an adaptive mutant, but what is distinct about electronic literature as opposed to print literature is that it cannot be accessed until it is performed by properly executed code. Due to the fundamental immediacy of the code to the text's performance, some genres of electronic literature have come to be known by the software or platform used to create, perform and access them such as Instapoetry.[1] Hayles (2007: Online) lists hypertext fiction, network fiction, interactive fiction, locative narratives, installation pieces, codework,[2] generative art and the Flash poem as the components that make up electronic literature. Flash was an interactive authoring software which used to be the professional application of choice for those wishing to produce online interactive animated content; however, because of a lack of compatibility with mobile devices it became less popular, and Adobe, its parent company, no longer develops new versions of it. This is a perfect example of how the speed of change in digital technologies also impacts digital poetry as a field, and as a result the terms used with reference to digital or digital poetry are vast and varied. For example, some of the terms I have come across in the course of my research (most notably in Funkhouser (2007) Simanowski (2011) Mencia (2017) and Rettberg (2019)) in relation to digital poetry are:

Text generators
Generators
Video text
Kinetic concrete poetry
Video
Auto
Digital videopoems
Animated poems
Generative
Computer poems
Digital poems
Digital videopoems

[1] Instapoetry is digital poetry found on Instagram, see Chap. 3, "Instapoetics and the Literary Algorithm," for more details.
[2] See Chap. 3, "Instapoetics and the Literary Algorithm," for an explanation of codework.

Hypertext poetry
Automatic poems
Visual poems
Interactive kinetic poetry

Hayles in her paper "The Time of Digital Poetry: From Object to Event" suggests that a digital poem is in fact a process, an event that is brought about through different factors such as software and hardware (Hayles 2006: 181). As in the Greek philosopher Heraclitus' belief that you cannot step in the same river twice, neither can the same digital poem be repeated as each time a process is carried out and variations in that process are inevitable (Hayles 2006: 186). Perhaps the platform or software is different; perhaps the machine lags. This differs to print poems in that though there is a process to arrive at the poem, once the end result is achieved they do not change, a printed poem is not an event in the sense that a digital poem is produced through and is an end result of programs being run each time the piece is loaded. There is a process to the production of the poem such as writing and printing however once the poem is printed and produced in a book or magazine its material structure does not noticeably change (Hayles 2006: 183). Aarseth (1997: 3) posits that cybertexts like digital poems are machines for the production of varieties of expression, in other words, there is in each piece the potential for a variety of different experiences. Unlike print where there is only one path and one potential though the nuances of the same may differ slightly depending on the reader and their unique experiences. Similarly, Funkhouser (2007: 234) describes digital poetry as many individual hybrid texts that can be seen to operate as a continuum on the Internet in their copresentation (Funkhouser 2007: 223). We can see therefore how digital poetry can be both a hybridic text and a process both online and offline and the mutability of digital texts is also important to note as texts are made of programmable bits that can be coded to take different forms. Janez Strehovec (2010: 71) tells us that in "the digital medium, the word loses its authority and solidity—which characterized its role in printed texts – and it appears as the raw material for numerous transformations and interventions." Flores (2013: 100) also references the mutability of digital texts as part of his suggested typology of digital texts and behaviours which includes Static texts, Scheduled texts, Kinetic texts, Responsive texts, Mutable texts and Aural texts. Flores (2013: 108) notes that mutability is not only a feature of digital poetry and cites Raymond Queneau's

1961 *Cent Mille Milliards de Poemes* which uses the book as a machine and the reader as an engine in order to create the potential for 100,000 billion sonnets. It was this work that prompted the collaboration between Raymond Queneau and the mathematician Francois de Lionnais which sparked the creation of the Ouvroir de Litterature Potentielle (OULIPO) group in 1960 (Funkhouser 2007: xxi–xxiv).

The fluidity and hybridic nature of the digital medium means that the definition of digital poetry is a complex and ever-changing task. Rettberg (2019: 118) terms digital poetry as kinetic and interactive poetry that explores "the specific multimedia capacities of the contemporary computer as a poetic environment for both composition and reception." Similarly Simanowski (2011: 58) uses the term kinetic concrete poetry, kinetic alludes to movement, moving poems. Concrete poetry however is poetry whose visual form mirrors the theme of the poem itself. Such as, a particular favourite of mine is *The Mouse's Tale* (Carroll 1993: 56), which appears in Lewis Carroll's (1865) *Alice's Adventures in Wonderland*. This is a poem that tells the story of a mouse through a poem that is visually presented in print in the form of a mouse's tail. Simanowski (2011: 58) contends, "kinetic concrete poetry remediates the poem in a manner more in line with the mainstream aesthetics of film and club culture." Correspondingly in certain examples of digital poetry we see movement providing a communicative value in much the same way as text and visuals. However, Simanowski's book *Digital Art and Meaning* approaches digital poetry from the art world and encompasses digital literature, kinetic concrete poetry, text machines, interactive installations, mapping art and real time web sculpture. Simanowski's (2011: x) analysis is contextualised by observing that, it is driven by "the belief that the first purpose that a digital work serves is to produce an act of creative expression." He invokes Sontag's (1964) essay *Against Interpretation* and Gumbrecht's (1994) essay *A Farewell to Interpretation* towards the task of developing an erotic hermeneutics of art (Simanowski 2011: 208–209).

The term kinetic is useful for digital poetry but once more this is a term that seeks to situate digital poetry within the field of early experimentation in visual media such as Anna Marie Uribe (Coverly 2017 in Mencia 2017: 7). Furthermore, given computers create and operate within the digital medium which is interactive, by its very nature using the term interactive along with the word digital is a tautology. This is why this book prefers to distil the term down quite simply to digital poetry, it is poetry and it is digital, seeking to expand the term even further can open the door to muddying the borders of an already highly hybridic form so all critical discussions become burdened with the task of self-justification and defence.

Shanmugapriya et al. (2019) propose the use of the term *technoeikon* to recognise the functions of embedded literary artifacts in digital literary works. They also refer to kinetic texts but also kinetic images, graphical designs, sounds and videos. They cite Genette's (1997) theory of para-texts, and they argue that in electronic literature these digital components have different digital ecology strategic pattern compared to, for example, the more easily identifiable components of other traditional literary texts such as preface, author's name, illustrations and title.

The emphasis on the word kinetic in much of the discussion of digital poetry would lead us to believe that movement as visual effect is character-istic of digital poetry that is not present in analogue poetry. Correspondingly it could be argued that the presence of this dimension (motion) is essential for the recognition of a piece as a digital poem. The word "kinetic" here signifies movement or motion, without such motion the poetry simply mirrored the print medium, that is, static and unmoving, irrespective of whether it included images or just text. So, motion is present, visual and audio elements are similarly most usually present but not necessarily always co-present. However contemporary examples of digital poetry would counter this as a defining characteristic, for example poetry made by a machine-learning algorithm does not necessarily contain movement. It is poetry that could only have been made using a digital apparatus so there-fore by that contention it is a digital poem. It can be printed out, does that mean it is still a digital poem?

According to this reasoning, without movement the apparatus is merely recreating the poem in its analogue form. Despite the fact that this is being done by the computer, a simulation machine, as per Hayles (2004: 71), by recreating the static analogue form it is not utilising the potential of the medium, that is the dynamic processes of which the computer is capable. Notably this concurs with the ELO's (Online) explanation of the term electronic literature. "The term refers to works with important liter-ary aspects that take advantage of the capabilities and contexts provided by the stand-alone or networked computer" (ELO: Online). However as per this logic without movement a poem is not a digital poem, it is a poem with audio and/or visuals, it is static as it is in print. Therefore it is not a digital poem, however it has been created by the apparatus namely the computer, a simulation machine.

Consequently by virtue of having been created by the simulation machine a digital poem is therefore a simulation. So as per postmodernist discourse it is a simulation of a representation. Therefore, a piece without movement that has been created and is experienced through a computer is still a digital poem, as it is still a simulation of a representation. Subsequently motion is not an essential characteristic of digital poetry but the apparatus is. Therefore this reasoning in fact accounts more completely for all potential kinds of digital poetry that could be encountered, most probably online but also possibly hidden away on an unknown digital poet's hard drive somewhere in the world. As per this logic a digital poem may, for example, consist of only visuals and motion but contain no interactivity.

Alternatively a digital poem may consist of visuals and interactivity but no motion, or even just visuals, yet by dint of it being created and experienced on the computer it is still recognised as a digital poem. Granted, it may not be an engaging or affective digital poem, but this research is not overly concerned with value judgments regarding digital poetry. Rather it is more concerned with understanding the process of its creation and resulting implications on form and meaning making in the digital space. This revised digital poetry rhetoric then corresponds more closely to Jenny Weight's description of her work. "My work Concatenation is a text-as-apparatus. It was necessarily created within, and necessarily experienced via the computer" (Weight 2006: 417). Despite the fact that Weight proposes this definition in relation to generative digital poetry we can now see that it can be applied to all types of digital poetry.

This logic however raises another question. If motion is not a defining characteristic of digital poetry but the apparatus is, then what about a poem written in Microsoft Word? Could this in itself constitute a digital poem? As long as it is being accessed on the computer, then yes, it is a digital poem. If the poem in Microsoft Word has links within it to a web site or to another document, then it is clearly a digital poem at its most basic level. However, if it does not then it could equally have been created without the apparatus, so it is not a digital poem.

Nonetheless when viewing a poem in Microsoft Word on the computer the human interpreter[3] has the option of deleting or moving words if they wish, an option not available to them in print. This corresponds to Vos' (2007: 199) view that digital poetry is "innovative poetry created and

---

[3] See Chap. 3, "Instapoetics and the Literary Algorithm," for an explanation and discussion of the term human interpreter.

experienced within the environment of new communication and information technologies—and it could not have been created nor cannot be experienced in other environments." As soon as the poem is printed it is no longer a digital poem, it has been transformed into an analogue poem. In this case it should be recognised that the apparatus is used as a tool for the creation of a poem but is not essential for accessing it. Therefore, the apparatus that is an essential feature of digital poetry is not the Internet, it is not Microsoft Word, it is not WordPress, it is in fact the computer. As Murray (2012: 8) states, "calling objects made with computing technology 'new' media obscures the fact that it is the computer that is the defining difference not the novelty." Logically then it is also clear that humans are also an essential characteristic of digital poetry as in order for the computer to run it needs a human to press a button.

This logic then expands considerably the definition of a digital poem. If every poem written and viewed in Word is a digital poem then there are many more digital poems in existence than initially anticipated. Much contemporary poetry is written directly onto a computer, but it is unknown how much of it is ever printed out. Bassett (2010: 145) references Hayles (2008: 43) in suggesting that the printing out of a poem "is simply one way to view what is already a digital text." The apparatus may perform in unanticipated ways along with the added variable of the human interpreter now becoming active in determining the actual form of the poem. When we also add to this the increased range of elements that the digital poets now have at their disposal (sound effects, links, music, text, buttons, colours, images, motion graphics, mixed reality immersive environments) it means that in digital poetry there exists many more potential variations in levels of meaning than in traditional analogue poetry. The following chapters attempt to explore this expanded potential for poetic expression in the context of contemporary innovative technologies.

SUMMARY

This chapter has drawn heavily on members of the ELO in order to give a brief history of digital poetry by referring to existing studies and research organisations concerned with the study of digital literature and digital poetry. This chapter then sought to define what digital poetry is by outlining the problematics of definition of a field that is inherently technocentric, hybridic and constantly changing in order to set the groundwork for the following chapters of this book. The defining elements of a digital

2 WHAT IS DIGITAL POETRY? 23

poem were also discussed in order to conclude that movement, audio, visuals and interactivity are not always required to be present in order to identify a digital poem, rather instead and crucially a digital poem is one that could only have been made using a computer and is more usefully identified as a process (as per Hayles 2006: 181). This chapter elucidated how digital poetry identification and definition are an endless task given the constantly changing landscape of digital technology. Many digital poetry forms that had been identified by the software that produced them are now no longer viewable such as *Adobe Flash* content because the software is no longer being developed. Other digital poetry examples such as *Instapoetry* are identified in relation to the platform they exist on as I will discuss in more detail in Chap. 3, "Instapoetics and the Literary Algorithm."

Aarseth, E. 1997. *Cybertext: Perspectives on Ergodic Literature*. Baltimore and London: Johns Hopkins University Press.
Amerika, M. 2007. *Meta/Data: A Digital Poetics*. Cambridge, MA: The MIT Press.
Bassett, C. 2010. Digital Media. *The Year's Work in Critical and Cultural Theory* 18: 139–154.
Bolter, J.D. 2001. *Writing Space: Computers, Hypertext, and the Remediation of Print*. Mahwah, NJ: Lawrence Erlbaum Associates.
Bootz, P. 1999. Alire: A Relentless Literary Investigation. *Electronic Book Review*, 15 March. Accessed 8 September 2015. electronicbookreview.com/thread/wuc/parisian.
Bootz, P., and S. Baldwin. 2010. *Regards Croisés*. Morgantown: West Virginia University Press.
Bootz, P., and H. Salceda. 2014. *Litterature et Numerique: quand, comment, pourquoi?* Paris: Presses Universitaires du Nouveau Monde.
Bouchardon, S. 2009. *Littérature numérique: Le récit interactif*. Paris: Hermes Science Publications.
Carroll, L. 1993. *Alice's Adventures in Wonderland & Through the Looking Glass*. Hertfordshire: Wordsworth Editions Limited.
Coverly, M.D. 2017. Women Innovate: Contributions to Electronic Literature (1990–2010). In *#WomenTechLit*, ed. M. Mencia. Morgantown: West Virginia University Press.
Electronic Literature Organisation. n.d. Online. Accessed 7 September 2020. https://eliterature.org/about/120/.
Emerson, L. 2014. *Reading Writing Interfaces: From the Digital to the Bookbound*. Minneapolis: University of Minnesota Press.

Flores, L. 2013. Digital Textuality and Its Behaviors. *Journal of Comparative Literature and Aesthetics* 36(1–2): 97+. Gale Academic OneFile. Accessed 2 October 2020. https://link.gale.com/apps/doc/A411197582/AONE?u=nu im&sid=AONE&xid=49a40964.

Funkhouser, C.T. 2007. *Prehistoric Digital Poetry: An Archaeology of Forms, 1959–1995*. Alabama: The University of Alabama Press.

Genette, G. 1997. *Paratexts: Thresholds of Interpretation*. Edited by J.E. Lewin and R.A. Macksey. New York, NY: Cambridge University Press.

Glazier, L.P. 2002. *Digital Poetics: The Making of E-Poetries*. Alabama: The University of Alabama Press.

Grigar, D. 2014. Curating Electronic Literature as Critical and Scholarly Practice. In *Digital Humanities Quarterly* 8(4). Accessed 14 September 2020. http://www.digitalhumanities.org/dhq/vol/8/4/000194/000194.html.

Hayles, N.K. 2004. Print Is Flat, Code Is Deep: The Importance of Media-Specific Analysis. *Poetics Today* 25 (1): 67–90.

———. 2006. The Time of Digital Poetry: From Object to Event. In *New Media Poetics: Contexts, Technotexts, and Theories*, ed. A. Morris and T. Swiss. Cambridge, MA: The MIT Press.

———. 2007. *Electronic Literature: What Is It?* Accessed 15 September 2020. http://www.eliterature.org/pad/elp.html.

———. 2008. *Electronic Literature: new horizons for the literary*. Indiana: University of Notre Dame.

———. 2012. *How We Think, Digital Media and Contemporary Technogenesis*. Chicago: University of Chicago Press.

Kac, E., ed. 1996. New Media Poetry: Poetic Innovation and New Technologies. [A Special Issue of] *Visible Language* 30(2): 137pp. ISSN 0022-2224.

Landow, G. 2006. *Hypertext 3.0 Critical Theory and new Media in an Era of Globalization*. 3rd ed. Maryland: The John Hopkins University Press.

Mencia, M., ed. 2017. *#WomenTechLit*. Morgantown: West Virginia University Press.

Murray, J. 2012. *Inventing the Medium: Principles of Interaction Design as a Cultural Practice*. Cambridge, MA: The MIT Press.

O'Sullivan, J. 2019. *Towards a Digital Poetics: Electronic Literature & Literary Games*. Accessed 16 August 2020. http://www.amazon.co.uk/kindlestore.

Rettberg, S. 2019. *Electronic Literature*. Cambridge: Polity.

Roberts, S. 2017. Online. Accessed 18 July 2020. https://www.newyorker.com/tech/annals-of-technology/christopher-stracheys-nineteen-fifties-love-machine.

Shanmugapriya, T., N. Menon, and A. Campbell. 2019. An Introduction to the Functioning Process of Embedded Paratext of Digital Literature: *Technoeikon* of Digital Poetry. *Digital Scholarship in the Humanities* 34 (3): 646–660. https://doi.org/10.1093/llc/fqy064.

Simanowski, R. 2011. *Digital Art and Meaning: Reading Kinetic Poetry*. Minneapolis: University of Minnesota Press.

Strehovec, J. 2010. Alphabet on the Move. In *Reading Moving Letters: Digital Literature in Research and Teaching. A Handbook*, ed. R. Simanowski, J. Schäfer, and P. Gendolla. London: Transaction Publishers.

———. 2016. *Text as Ride*. Morgantown: Computing Literature.

Tabbi, J. 2017. *Bloomsbury Handbook of Electronic Literature*. London: Bloomsbury.

Vos, E. 2007. Media Poetry—Theories and Strategies. In *Media Poetry, an International Anthology*, ed. E. Kac, 199–212. Bristol and Chicago: Intellect Books.

Wardrip-Fruin, N. 2005. *Christopher Strachey: The First Digital Artist?* Grand Text Auto. School of Engineering, University of California Santa Cruz. Accessed 19 August 2020. https://grandtextauto.soe.ucsc.edu/2005/08/01/christopher-strachey-first-digital-artist/.

Weight, J. 2006. I, Apparatus, You: A Technosocial Introduction to Creative Practice. *Convergence: The International Journal of Research into New Media Technologies* 12 (4): 413–446.

CHAPTER 3

Instapoetics and the Literary Algorithm

Abstract This chapter will look at examples of machine learning poetry and Instagram poetry in order to examine the cultural impact of a posthuman cyborgian fluidity of borders as audiences expand and algorithms cannibalise texts and spew out literary artefacts. Discussions will incorporate a post humanism lens stemming from N. K. Hayles (*How We Became Posthuman: Virtual Bodies in Cybernetics, Literature, and Informatics*, Chicago: University of Chicago Press, 1999), John Cayley (The Code Is Not the Text (Unless It Is the Text). *Electronic Book Review*, 2002) and Karoliina Lummaa (Posthumanist Reading: Witnessing Ghosts, Summoning Nonhuman Powers. In *Reconfiguring Human, Nonhuman and Posthuman in Literature and Culture*, ed. S. Karkulehto, A. Koistinen, and E. Varis. New York and London: Routledge, 41–56, 2020). Both machine learning and Instagram poetry can be classified as anthropophagic algorithmic texts—cannibalistic algorithm-driven texts that remix, reuse and re-appropriate content—and specific examples can show us how non-human participation in digital poetry is established. I will include discussions and statistics regarding the audience demographics of Instagram and what implication this might potentially have for the future of poetry.

Keywords Posthumanism • Posthumanities • Poetry • Instapoetry • Cyborgs • Algorithms

© The Author(s), under exclusive license to Springer Nature Switzerland AG 2021
J. Naji, *Digital Poetry*, https://doi.org/10.1007/978-3-030-65962-2_3

27

Technology has always been involved in reading and writing but now in the second age of machines we are not only using technology to inscribe and encode but to remember and write.[1] For example, Samuel Gibbs in *The Guardian* tells about Google's artificial intelligence project that is writing poetry, a by-product of research into enhancing the natural language skills of the recurrent neural network language model. The algorithm was provided with thousands of romance novels and the system was then given starting and ending sentences and asked to fill in the gap (Gibbs 2016: Online). Jack Hopkins also developed a poetic bot at the University of Cambridge that was a neural network trained on thousands of lines of poetry (Reynolds 2017: Online). Leonardo Flores (2018) suggests that the contemporary digital landscape of sharing, copying, pasting, linking and remixing of content to massive audiences and communities has spawned a new category of electronic literature, what he refers to as third-generation literature. According to Flores (2018), third-generation literature works in spaces with massive audiences. Instagram and machine learning poetry are examples of algorithmically driven third-generation electronic literature that can demonstrate massive audiences and remixed content that are usefully examined through a posthuman lens towards the goal of understanding human subjectivities in cyberspace.

THE POSTHUMANITIES AND POETRY

Posthumanism is a contemporary wide-reaching theoretical framework that I can't hope to cover in its entirety in this short chapter. Cary Wolfe makes a valiant attempt in his 2009 *What is Posthumanism?* and he talks of how posthumanism engages "directly with the problem of anthropocentrism and speciesism and how practices of thinking and reading must change in light of their critique" (Wolfe 2009: xix). A few years later in 2013 Herbrechter's publication *Posthumanism: A Critical Analysis* addresses the concept of a techno-centric transformation of humans, a posthumanisation as he terms it. When discussing posthumanism it is difficult to steer away from utopian notions of humans surpassing themselves through a digital liberation of our baser fallible organic beings. This chapter seeks not to replicate such naive approaches to technology, which can

---

[1] See Chap. 7, "Conclusion: Future Poetics: Literary Expression in the Second Age of machines," for discussion regarding the second age of machines.

cost us as much as we gain, however it must be acknowledged that technology has transformed us, digital technology more so. As Morris suggests
that "from a posthuman point of view, we are not the bounded, autonomous, coherent, and fully self-conscious beings imagined by Enlightenment
thinkers, but cybernetic organisms joined in a continuous feedback loops
with media and information technologies" (Morris and Swiss 2006: 4).
So, in this not only is the technology essential but so too are we. Morris is
expanding what N. Katherine Hayles (1999) terms the "post human" era
as we all are increasingly continually connected and hence defined by digital influences both in media and elsewhere. We can no longer talk of *the
machine* impersonally when we are in fact connected to and part of it,
directing the flowing of digital data. Wolfe (2009: xv) sees Hayles' (1999)
seminal approach to posthumanism as opposing the idea of embodiment
with machines in favour of a "triumphant disembodiment" with machines
that is not anti-human. Wolfe (2009: xv) however uses the opposite sense
of the term towards embodiment but still in opposition to traditional
humanist "fantasies of disembodiment and autonomy" and in that sense is
still posthumanist.

In all cases poetic expression in the digital medium has come a great
distance from the realm of traditional poetry. What we find are the essential characteristics of what might be termed the postmodern, to borrow
from David Harvey (1990), and posthuman, to borrow from N. Katherine
Hayles (1999), condition referring to the pervasive sense of fragmenta-
tion, loss of individuality, roots and connection characteristic of the postmodern world and the equally pervasive awareness that one's own
self-identity intellectual, emotional, biological and of course interpersonal
functioning is now ever bound up in the digital poetry experience.
Interestingly this can be linked to what Paul de Man (in Brower 1970:
157) tells us of Yeats' belief regarding modern poetry "as the conscious
expression of a conflict within the function of language as representation
and within the conception of language as the act of an autonomous self"
(Brower 1970: 157).

Andrew Dewdney and Peter Ride in *The New Media Handbook*
(Dewdney and Ride 2006: 305) also discuss the idea of the post-human,
and note in particular its use with reference to accounting for the recon-
figuration of human subjectivities in cyberspace. In this instance the posthuman is used to elucidate how human identity is changed through
interaction with the apparatus. Dewdney and Ride reference Haraway
(1991), Plant (2000) and Hayles (2002) in terms of extensions to the

discussions of post-human which also deal with humans' cultural and psychological response to a world in which a "networked cybernetic system is installed as the medium of communication and knowledge" (Hayles in Dewdney and Ride 2006: 30).

Karoliina Lummaa (2020) offers a posthuman close reading of the Finnish poem "a niinkuin koira" [a as a dog] by Dan Waber and Marko Niemi and recognises the flickering signifiers (as per Hayles 1999: 31) of its signs. Lummaa outlines how there are a number of algorithms working to bring the digital poem to life in a dynamic way that cannot be recreated on a printed page. In conducting any close reading of digital poetry, it is important to remember Hayles' (1999) concept of a flickering signifier. In the digital space a signifier according to Hayles "can no longer be understood as a single marker, for example an ink mark on a page. Rather it exists as a flexible chain of markers bound together by the arbitrary relations specified by the relevant codes" (Hayles 1999: 31). A posthumanist position not only recognises the dynamic and fluid nature of semiotic codes but also recognises the presence of non-human agents in the reading and writing process. Similarly Wolfe (2009: 6) incorporates discussions of nonhuman elements in posthumanism as his book sees communication extending beyond the human to nonhuman animals and exceeds "the boundary between the living and the mechanical or technical." Another theoretical framework that can be used to account for multiple hermeneutic agents is the Actor Network Theory which proposes that any social process involves both human and non-human actors with their own agencies (Latour 2005: 128). Posthumanism however offers an insight into the changing human subjectivities in cyberspace that we traditionally expect the humanities to interpret for us. This is why in a posthuman digital poem we have the perfect object to symbolise the shifting dynamics of human identities, relationships and methods of communication and meaning making.

Donna Haraway's 1991 paper "The Cyborg Manifesto: Science, Technology, and Socialist-Feminism in the Late Twentieth Century" (Haraway 1991: 149–181) is an essential text to mention here with reference to the concept of the posthuman. Haraway believes a "cyborg exists when two kinds of boundaries are simultaneously problematic: 1) that between animals (or other organisms) and humans, and 2) that between self-controlled, self-governing machines (automatons) and organisms, especially humans (models of autonomy). The cyborg is a figure born of the interface of automaton and autonomy" (Haraway 1991: 139). Aarseth

(1997: 54) suggests that the most significant part of Haraway's theory is the relationship of organism and machine which, thanks to new technologies, challenges the traditional concepts of Western humanism inspired by "Michel Foucault's claim that 'man is an invention of a recent date. And one perhaps nearing its end' (Foucault 1973, 387; see also Springer 1991, 322)" (Aarseth 1997: 54).

INSTAPOETICS

Nowhere is this intertwining of human subjectivities and networked algorithms of the machine more apparent than in Instapoetry, a multimodal socio-technical literary artefact. Understanding who actually uses Instagram is an important component of developing any theory of *Instapoetics* and any analysis of literary algorithms.

Instagram User Data

The Pew Research Center's 2013 Social Media Update research tells us that 17% of all American Internet users use Instagram of which 20% are women, 15% are men, 34% are Non-Hispanic Black, 23% are Hispanic and just 12% are white, Non-Hispanic. Furthermore 37% of American Instagram users in 2013 are aged 18–29 compared to just 18% of 30–49 year olds, 6% of 50–64 year olds and 1% are those over the age of 65. Most American Instagram users have some college, earn between $30,000 and $49,000 and live in urban areas (Duggan and Smith 2013). This data suggests that the average American Instagram users are Non-Hispanic Black, aged 18–29 with some college, and they live in urban areas and earn between $30,000 and $49,000. This is not dissimilar to the average user profile of Twitter users however twitter users are 18% women and 17% men. Facebook user data has a much wider spread with no noticeable large differential between genders and ages and ethnicity except for less users over the age of 65. Therefore the significant difference of Instagram users compared to other social media users is that it was used more by American women between the ages of 18 and 29 in 2013 (Duggan and Smith 2013). The website NapoleonCat (n.d.: Online) does provide some European data and statistics on social media users with the proviso that their data is sourced from Facebook's advertising system and therefore does not constitute official Instagram stats. Given the commercial nature of social media platforms most statistics on users is in fact a valuable commodity and therefore not freely available. However, looking at the data that NapoleonCat (2015) does provide, we can see that it corresponds to the trends of the American Pew research data which indicates that of the 17 European countries[2] analysed it was found that in most countries there are more female Instagram users except for Turkey where 61% of Instagram users are male and in Germany where the breakdown of Instagram users is 50% males and 50% females. The majority of Instagram users in Europe also fall into the 18–24 age category except for Spain where the majority of Instagram users are aged 25–34.

The mainly female demographic of Instapoetry's readers and writers is notable not least because of the way it is often dismissed and denigrated in literary circles. In the Jan–Feb 2018 edition of the *PN Review* Rebecca Watts wrote "The Cult of the Noble Amateur" in which she describes "the rise of a cohort of young female poets who are currently being lauded by the poetic establishment for their 'honesty' and 'accessibility'—buzzwords for the open denigration of intellectual engagement and rejection of craft that characterises their work." In her article, she quotes work from Instagram poet Rupi Kaur's 2015 title *Milk and Honey* published by Andrews McMeel publishing. In the same article, Rebecca Watts (2018) states that "of all the literary forms, we might have predicted that poetry had the best chance of escaping social media's dumbing effect; its project, after all, has typically been to rid language of cliché. Yet in the redefinition of poetry as 'short-form communication' the floodgates have been opened. The reader is dead: long live consumer-driven content and the 'instant gratification' this affords". Criticism such as this corresponds with what Thomas (2020: 89–90) accounts regarding female poets known primarily for their work on Instagram, such as Rupi Kaur (4 million followers), Charly Cox (44k followers) and Lang Leav (543k followers) being criticised for writing "self-indulgent pieces, or for wallowing in their own misery." Bronwen Thomas (2020: 90) reminds us that there exists a long history of female writers being attached for being too "emotional, some things, it would appear, never change." This shows that consideration of gender is an important component in the formation of a theory of Instapoetics.

Carl Wilson suggests that Instagram poetry could be the birth of young adult poetry like a midway point between children's poetry and adult

[2] The 17 countries include the United Kingdom who were part of the European Union at the time of NapoleonCat's 2015 analysis.

poetry (BBC Radio 4: 2018). A *Guardian* article written in February 2016 by Michelle Dean entitled "Instagram Poets Society: Selfie Age Gives New Life and Following into Poetry" rebuffs David Denby who wrote a New Yorker article concerned that younger generations were not reading the "Classics" of great literature. Dean quotes from the comments section of popular Instagram poet @Atticus in which his readers list their top ten poets and "classic" names such as "Orwell, Flannery O'Connor, Sylvia Plath, Khalil Gibran and Maya Angelou" appear. Dean (2016) also points out that Instagram poets are often also Tumblr and Pinterest poets; these are all social media channels that amass huge audiences of reading communities that share, remix and recirculate content continuously. Remixing culture is therefore a recognisable precursor and current component of Instapoetry in a posthuman hybridity of form.

Instapoetry is also clearly multimodal with as much an emphasis on the visual as on the text, and the "reader" responses can become as much a part of the poetic experience as the multimodal artefact authored by the poet. What is interesting about Instapoetry is that it operates by continuously remixing and recirculating; content, responses, likes and remixes are elicited so that the form invites participation in a manner similar to Delwiche and Henderson's (2012) theories regarding participatory culture and discussion communities. So, for example, many users will requote Instapoets such as Nikita Gill (578 k followers) and Atticus (1.5 million followers) while sharing one of their own images or even their own poetry with the hashtag #nikitagill or #atticus to reference the quote and/or the poet. This can provide a new dimension of meaning to a couple of lines of poetry and often personalise the experience for members of the community. Critiquing Instagram by focusing only on the words as is done with print poetry is like evaluating an elephant based on its trunk, we are missing a large part of the animal, in this case its socio-technical apparatus and networks (Naji 2018: 5).

Another important component of Instapoetry's socio-technical apparatus is the algorithm, or should I say the algorithms, as there are a multitude of software at play in each Instapoetry experience. Simanowski (2010: 162) tells us that it is the materiality of text in digital media that is focused on which can often undermine its linguistic signification. To look at, for example, contemporary screen-based Instagram poetry, the poetic words become part of the image, subsumed and cannibalised into a primarily visual semiotic framework. In these instances, it is the words that we traditionally identify as poetry, it is the words that differentiate these Instagram posts from others to make them identifiable as poetry and yet it is the words that get subsumed into what Kress (2003: 7) terms the logic of the image.[3]

Thomas (2020: 8) cites Genette's (1997) idea of the paratext that referred to all materials in relation to a literary text such as the blurb, prefaces and commentaries. In contemporary usage this can be a useful concept to remind us to look beyond the confines of a single text in order to take into account discussions of context and audience. I suggest instead adopting a more detailed approach that also embraces the socio-technical materialities of digital texts in order to not only consider context and audiences but also software and algorithms. This approach follows Hayles' (2004) argument regarding the importance of a media-specific analysis, as to date the most innovative digital cultural analysis methodologies proposed are those for the Internet, a medium that has already been in existence for quite some time and only now is becoming widely accepted as a legitimate avenue for cultural analysis and research. This lag is unfortunate given the multimodal frameworks such as those proposed by Pauwels (2012) for the analysis of websites as cultural expressions are already dated now that we are moving away from the screen into immersive environments. While many of these frameworks recognise cyberspace as a complex techno-cultural environment that can be seen to be multi-authored and hybrid (Pauwels 2012: 249), they fail to adequately recognise the impact of the myriad techno-social agents at play and the materiality and affordances of the media in which they operate. Jarrett and Naji (2016) propose social media literary texts as assemblages of interactions between technologies, human creative subjects and wider socioeconomic contexts. They propose exploring memes, videos, tweets or blog posts as instances of technosocial communication that foreground the interplay of text, algorithms and users. Jarrett and Naji (2016) argue for moving beyond explorations of signification to understanding the unfixed, processual qualities of these texts, including exploring them through the affective experiences of production and consumption.

---

[3] I expand on Kress' multimodal theories in relation to how words operate in virtual spaces in Chap. 6, "Poetic Mirror Worlds and Mixed Reality Poetry."

THE LITERARY ALGORITHM

Discussions so far in this chapter have highlighted the complexity of processes at play in Instapoetry and have made it clear that in order to move towards developing a critical theory of Instapoetics through a posthuman lens it is important to recognise all socio-technical agents in the literary process. One element that needs to be recognised is the audience which is mainly non-white and female who are creating remixed artifacts with increasingly complex and varied algorithmical processes at play. Not only are Instapoetry's audiences unique but so too are the algorithms which also need to be recognised as agents, could we identify them as literary algorithms? What could be considered a literary algorithm? Does it differ from other algorithms in ways other than function? Manovich (2011: Online) refers to "cultural software - cultural in the sense that it is directly used by hundreds and millions of people and that it carries 'atoms' of culture (media and information, as well as human interactions around these media and information)" (Manovich 2011: Online). Alternatively, Simanowski (2011: vii) suggests that, "a preoccupation with code threatens to divert our attention from the actual meaning of an artifact. It encourages claims such as the notion that everything in digital media is actually literature because everything is represented as alphanumeric code."

The algorithm, of course, is no stranger to poetry and the terms *computational poetry* and *codework* were included in the fourth edition of *Princeton Encyclopedia of Poetry and Poetics* (Cushman et al. 2012). In it, Morris (Cushman et al. 2012: 288) explains that computational poems are unlike organic or formalist poems, in that a computational poem is produced and enacted by a procedure in which the poem's form acts as its intelligence. Codework (Morris in Cushman et al. 2012: 271) is noted as being coined by Sondheim in 2001 and is defined as "a term used by new media practitioners and theorists to describe digital writing in which normally invisible lang. addressed to a computer's operating system appears on the screen with lang. addressed to human interpreters" (Cushman et al. 2012: 271).

Jenny Weight (2006: 414) also uses the phrase human interpreters and argues that we must consider not only the apparatus (hardware) and the algorithm (software) but also the human interpreter (wetware) (Morris 2006: 8). Machine learning poetry examples are useful for this next stage of discussion as unique and contemporary literary artifacts whose algorithms have more agency in the technosocial process than any previous examples of digital poetry in that they can learn and generate original content. Text generators perhaps could be considered precursors to machine learning poetry in that text generators used an algorithm to create text; however, machine learning literature means that the algorithm "reads" a certain type of literature in order to "learn" from it and then produces original text in that same style. This could also be argued as an example of a remixed literary artifact given the machine is learning from previous examples; however, the remixing is less explicit as you would find in Instapoetry. I would argue that gender politics should also be considered as machine learning arising from the domain of the sciences could be seen as being white male dominated. In 2018 *Wired* magazine in collaboration with ElementAI estimated that just 12% of leading machine learning researchers were women (Wired 2018: Online). In 2019 the AI Now Institute published a report that flagged the diversity problem in the AI industry as a serious problem which results in AI continuing to perpetuate existing structural inequalities (Synced 2020: Online).

Algorithms remain at the core of all digital poetry, and an algorithm is basically a series of instructions. Weight (2006) describes algorithms as interactivity; in other words, the algorithm dictates the extent to which the human interpreter is given freedom within the environment. Algorithms link the user to the database allowing them to form new relationships (Weight 2006: 431–432). Correspondingly Strehovec (2010: 64) contends that digital poetry is enabled by software as a cultural tool. Alternatively, Simanowski (2011: vii) suggests that, "a preoccupation with code threatens to divert our attention from the actual meaning of an artifact. It encourages claims such as the notion that everything in digital media is actually literature because everything is represented as alphanumeric code." Nonetheless, Watten (2006: 365) suggests that in digital media art the methods of communication are the communication and digital art is both visual display and textual coding. We can see this also reflects McLuhan's (1964) theory, regarding the medium as the message, in that the communication takes place through both the visuals that the computer creates by processing the code, and also through the code itself. So for the purposes of this research, we can see that digital poetry not only communicates through visual and textual language on screen but also through code and language. Any trilogical relationship such as that between the apparatus, the programmer and the interpreter has an inherent conflict between two models of language, the programming language and natural language. Ong (2002: 7) believes that while computer languages seem to resemble human languages in certain manners (in that they have rules, such as grammar) they are in fact completely different. This according to Ong (2002: 7) is due to their noetic nature, in that they come straight from human consciousness, whereas human language comes straight from the unconscious.

Jenny Weight's online creative poetic work belongs to a sub-genre called generative poetics. This work is textual with regards to both the programming and the surface display. Weight calls such texts "text-as-apparatus" and outlines their ultimate purpose "is to promote environments in which interpretation happens" (Weight 2006: 416). Weight (2006: 419) defines programming as "a species of logical writing whose operational efficacy derives from the correspondence of surface display … with coded instruction, where correspondence is not equivalent to representation." What is significant for any apparatus or executing code is that it can be executed without error. Code can only ever 'signify' one thing. It is not open to interpretation. The apparatus has no concept of multiplicity; there is no 'beyond' the data, when a computer encounters a 'bug' in the code, no dialogic negotiation takes place. The programme—the performance—stops (Weight 2006: 420). With reference to this John Cayley in his paper "The Code is not the Text (Unless It Is the Text)" (Cayley 2002: Online) also uses the term codework. He describes this term as it applies to literature which "uses, addresses, and incorporates code as an underlying language-animating or language-generating programming." Cayley (2002: Online) views this as a special type of language in itself, or as an intrinsic part of the new surface language or "interface text" of writing in networked and programmable media. Manovich states that the "act of writing code itself is very important, regardless of what this code actually does at the end" (2006: 216). Though the apparatus is considered a partner in this undertaking and the texts cannot be understood separately from this apparatus, the interpretation only takes part on the side of the human user. In short computers cannot read poetry only humans can. "The apparatus does not care that representations of linear connection are somewhat emblematic of the human condition" (Weight 2006: 433), that meaning or significance is ever framed by a need to make narrative connections they simply determine what narrative connections will be possible. It is only the human element in this relationship that has a need to construct meaning, a need for meaning which remains at the heart of digital poetry, just as it has forever been with traditional poetry. It is not surprising that meaning is central to the creation of all poetry, however natural language is not a transparent bearer of meaning in the way that programming code absolutely must be. "Natural language works on principles of coherence, empathy and a level of syntactical forgiveness" (Weight 2006: 419). Natural language is always concerned with meaning, which is contextualised and nuanced. It emerges from the way specific individuals interpret the unity of the text into a multiplicity of elements, and then unify it again. When humans encounter an apparently nonsensical piece of text (such as a "bug" to a programmed apparatus) they usually attempt to extrapolate some meaning through clues and cues (Weight 2006: 420).

Unlike the apparatus, the human interpreter engages in a "back and forth" between the unity of text and multiple factors in the world that might be brought to bear on interpretation, the interpreter cannot help reaching beyond the text, the apparatus has no capacity to do so. Morris (2006: 9) also lists three components of a digital poem, these are: the data fields (similar to Weight's database), the code (similar to Weight's algorithm) and the display (similar to Weight's interface). Stephanie Strickland (2006: Online) a theorist and digital poet also proposes that there exists three agents: writer-coder, machine processor-network and player-reader. She believes that unless all three of these peers are communicating and engaged then nothing is happening. This mirrors Weight's (2006) technosocial trilogical relationship of the machine, the algorithm and the apparatus which itself builds on Manovich's (2001) database and Flusser's (2000) apparatus. This trilogical technosocial relationship is clearly integral to understanding meaning making in digital poetry as it is essential that all contributors to the communicative process are considered.

Ryan Prewitt and Max Accardi presented *Poetry-by-Numbers: Exploring the Implications of Machine-Generated Instapoetry* at the Virtual Zoom #ReadingInstaPoetry Conference at the University of Glasgow which ran from the 14th to the 16th of July. This is a notable example to discuss in this chapter because it incorporates both machine learning and Instapoetry algorithms. Prewitt and Accardi noted that the rigid formal features and uniform, basic language of Instapoetry were also consistent with machine-generated texts. They compiled a corpus of roughly 5000 Instapoetry texts and developed an algorithm that learned from the formal qualities and linguistic associations found in the corpus and then generated representative Instapoetry using Natural Language Processing and statistical modelling techniques. Prewitt and Accardi's goal was to seek to understand the conditions of emerging digital literatures, and indeed, the results viewable at *vesper.rose.poems* on Instagram contribute to the genre.

Summary

The tension between code and language in the semiotic space of the techno-environment that it inhabits is filled with hermeneutic potential but the social dimensions of algorithmical poetry such as demographics and gender and race are essential components of any hermeneutical analysis. The semiotic modes need also to be considered not forgetting the visual and aural modes of communication and the interactive potential of the multimodal space. We are left with a networked environment in which meaning is formed in a dynamic way in relation to other actors within the network. The more I research digital poetry the more complex it becomes and the realisation that each different type of digital poetry requires different aspects to be considered because of the vastly differing socio-techno environments they inhabit.

Some aspects of digital poetry are similar no matter the socio-techno environment and it is perhaps those on which we should focus; the core commonality in all digital poetry processes would appear to be the algorithm and the human interpreter. Any definition of a literary algorithm therefore needs to be relational, as function, intention and interpretation have to be considered. The function of a literary algorithm and whether the human interpreter intended or interpreted a literary meaning from the process can define a literary algorithm. If the function of the code is to make a poem it can be considered a literary algorithm, or if the function of the code is not obviously literary but the intention of the human author was to create a literary object then it can be deemed a literary algorithm. Alternatively, if the human interpreter constructs literary meaning from the digital object even if the function and human author did not intend it then it too can be deemed a literary algorithm. So, a literary algorithm can be defined in relation to the intention of the human interpreter engaged in the digital poetry process.

References

Aarseth, E. 1997. *Cybertext: Perspectives on Ergodic Literature*. Baltimore and London: Johns Hopkins University Press.

BBC Radio 4. 2018. The Poetry of Instagram. https://www.bbc.co.uk/programmes/b09tcb4w (retrieved 12 April 2018).

Brower, R.A. 1970. Foreword. In *Forms of Lyric: Selected Papers from the English Institute*, ed. R.A. Brower. New York and London: Columbia University Press.

Cayley, J. 2002. The Code Is Not the Text (Unless It Is the Text). *Electronic Book Review*. Accessed 9 September 2020. http://electronicbookreview.com/ essay/the-code-is-not-the-text-unless-it-is-the-text/.

Cushman, S., C. Cavanagh, J. Ramazani, and P. Rouzer, eds. 2012. *The Princeton Encyclopedia of Poetry and Poetics*. 4th ed. Princeton: Princeton University Press.

Dean, M. 2016. 'Instagram poets society: selfie age gives new life and following into poetry'. https://www.theguardian.com/books/2018/jan/23/poetry-world-split-over-polemic-attacking-amateur-work-by-young-female-poets (retrieved 12 April 2018).

Delwiche, A., and Henderson, J. 2012. 'The Participatory Cultures Handbook'. London and New York: Routledge.

Dewdney, A., and P. Ride. 2006. *The New Media Handbook*. London and New York: Routledge.

Duggan, Maeve, and Aaron Smith. 2013. *Demographics of Key Social Networking Platforms*. Accessed 3 April 2020. https://www.pewresearch.org/internet/2013/12/30/demographics-of-key-social-networking-platforms/.

Flores, L. 2018. *Lecture: Third Generation Electronic Literature*. Accessed 12 April 2018. http://leonardoflores.net/blog/lecture-third- generation-electronic-literature/.

Flusser, V. 2000. *Towards a Philosophy of Photography*. London: Reaktion Books.

Foucault, Michel. 1973. The order of things; an archaeology of the human sciences. New York: Vintage Books.

Gibbs, S. 2016. *Google AI Project Writes Poetry Which Could Make a Vogon Proud*. Accessed 9 September 2020. https://www.theguardian.com/technology/2016/may/17/googles-ai-write-poetry-stark-dramatic-vogons.

Haraway, D.J. 1991. A Cyborg Manifesto: Science, Technology, and Socialist-Feminism in the Late Twentieth Century. In *Simians, Cyborgs and Women: The Reinvention of Nature*, 149–181. New York: Routledge.

Harvey, D. 1990. *The Condition of Postmodernity: An Enquiry into the Origins of Modern Change*. Massachusetts and Oxford: Wiley-Blackwell.

Hayles, N.K. 1999. *How We Became Posthuman: Virtual Bodies in Cybernetics, Literature, and Informatics*. Chicago: University of Chicago Press.

———. 2002. *Writing Machines*. Cambridge, MA: The MIT Press.

Hayles, N. Katherine. 2004. Print Is Flat, Code Is Deep: The Importance of Media-Specific Analysis. *Poetics Today* 25 (1): 67–90.

Herbrechter, S. 2013. *Posthumanism: A Critical Analysis*. London: Bloomsbury.

Jarrett, K., and J. Naji. 2016. What Would Media Studies Do? Social Media Shakespeare as a Technosocial Process. *Borrowers and Lenders: The Journal of Shakespeare and Appropriation*. http://www.borrowers.uga.edu/1794/show.

Kress, G. 2003. 'Literacy in the New Media Age'. London and New York: Routledge.

Latour, B. 2005. *Reassembling the Social: An Introduction to Actor-Network-Theory*. New York, NY: Oxford University Press.
Lummaa, K. 2020. Posthumanist Reading: Witnessing Ghosts, Summoning Nonhuman Powers. In *Reconfiguring Human, Nonhuman and Posthuman in Literature and Culture*, ed. S. Karkulehto, A. Koistinen, and E. Varis, 41–56. London and New York: Routledge.
Manovich, L. 2001. *The Language of New Media*. Cambridge, Massachusetts: MIT Press.
Manovich, L. 2006. Generation Flash. In: Chun, W.H.K. and Keenan, T. (eds.) New Media, old media: a history and theory reader. London and New York: Routledge.
Manovich, L. 2011. Cultural Software. Available at: http://manovich.net/content/04-projects/070-cultural-software/67-article-2011.pdf Accessed 19 February 2021.
McLuhan, Marshall. 1964 'Understanding Media: The Extensions of Man', New York: McGraw Hill.
Morris, A. 2006. New Media Poetics: As We May Think/How to Write. In: Morris, A. and Swiss, T. (eds.) New Media Poetics: contexts, technotexts, and theories. Cambridge, Massachusetts: The MIT Press.
Morris, A., and T. Swiss, eds. 2006. *New Media Poetics: Contexts, Technotexts, And Theories*. Cambridge, MA: The MIT Press.
Naji, J. 2018. The Posthuman Poetics of Instagram Poetry. In *EVA Copenhagen 2018—Politics of the Machines—Art and After*. https://doi.org/10.14236/ewic/EVAC18.1.
NapoleanCat. 2015. Accessed 15 July 2020. https://www.slideshare.net/cheese-cat/instagram-users-demographics-in-selected-european-countries.
———. n.d. Online. Accessed 15 July 2020. https://napoleoncat.com.
Ong, W.J. 2002. *Orality and Literacy*. New York: Routledge.
Pauwels, L. 2012. A Multimodal Framework for Analyzing Websites as Cultural Expressions. In: "Journal of Computer-Mediated Communication" 17 (2012) 247–265.
Plant, S. 2000. On the Matrix: Cyberfeminist Simulations. In *The Gendered Cyborg*, ed. G. Kirkup. London and New York: Routledge.
Reynolds, M. 2017. *Neural Network Poetry Is So Bad We Think It's Written by Humans*. Accessed 9 September 2020. https://www.newscientist.com/article/2140014-neural-network-poetry-is-so-bad-we-think-its-written-by-humans/.
Simanowski, R. 2010. *Digital Anthropophagy: Refashioning Words as Image, Sound and Action*. Leonardo 43(2), 159–163. The MIT Press. Accessed August 29, 2018. Project MUSE database.
———. 2011. *Digital Art and Meaning: Reading Kinetic Poetry*. Minneapolis: University of Minnesota Press.

Sondheim, A. 2001. Introduction: Codework. *American Book Review* 22(6): 1. Accessed 9 September 2020. http://litline.org/ABR/issues/Volume22/Issue6/sondheim.pdf.

Springer, C. 1991. The pleasure of the interface, Screen, Volume 32, Issue 3, Autumn 1991, Pages 303–323, https://doi.org/10.1093/screen/32.3.303

Strehovec, J. 2010, 'Alphabet on the Move' In Simanowski, R., Schäfer, J., Gendolla, P. (eds) Reading Moving Letters: Digital Literature in Research and Teaching. A Handbook, London: Transaction Publishers.

Strickland, S. 2006. Writing the Virtual: Eleven Dimensions of E-Poetry. *Leonardo Electronic Almanac* 14(5): pp. 11 March 2011. Accessed 9 September 2020. https://www.leoalmanac.org/wp-content/uploads/2012/09/06Writing-the-Virtual-Eleven-Dimensions-of-E-Poetry-by-Stephanie-Strickland-Vol-14-No-5-6-September-2006-Leonardo-Electronic-Almanac.pdf.

Synced AI Technology & Industry Review. 2020. *Exploring Gender Imbalance in AI: Numbers, Trends, and Discussions.* Accessed 9 September 2020. https://syncedreview.com/2020/03/13/exploring-gender-imbalance-in-ai-numbers-trends-and-discussions/.

Thomas, Bronwen. 2020. Literature and social media. London and New York: Routledge.

Watten, B. 2006. 'Poetics in the Expanded Field: Textual, Visual, Digital...'. In: Morris, A. and Swiss, T. (eds.) New Media Poetics: contexts, technotexts, and theories. Cambridge, Massachusetts: The MIT Press.

Watts, R. (2018) The Cult of the Noble Amateur. PN Review 239, Volume 44 Number 3, January - February 2018. https://www.pnreview.co.uk/cgi-bin/scribe?item_id=10090 (retrieved 12 April 2018).

Weight, J. 2006. I, Apparatus, You: A Technosocial Introduction to Creative Practice. *Convergence: The International Journal of Research into New Media Technologies* 12 (4): 413–446.

Wired. 2018. *AI Is the Future—But Where Are the Women?* Accessed 9 September 2020. https://www.wired.com/story/artificial-intelligence-researchers-gender-imbalance/.

Wolfe, C. 2009. *What Is Posthumanism?*, University of Minnesota Press, Minneapolis. Accessed 25 November 2020. ProQuest Ebook Central.

CHAPTER 4

Haptic Hermeneutics and Poetry Apps

Abstract This chapter seeks to establish the hermeneutic potential of haptic gesture within a theoretical framework that references examples of digital poetry apps on mobile platforms. The unique interpretative potential of literary objects on mobile devices is highlighted by incorporating haptic gesture into the hermeneutic framework, thereby potentially offering a more embodied literary experience. Contemporary examples of mobile electronic literature apps are referenced such as Pry by Gorman and Cannizzaro, Abra! by Amaranth Borsuk, Kate Durbin and Ian Hatcher (& You), and finally Jason Edwards Lewis and Bruno Nadeau's PoEMM. This chapter finds that despite the closed nature of mobile platforms, haptic hermeneutics can offer increased potential for an embodied literary experience.

Keywords Mobile poetry apps • Gestural meaning making • Haptic hermeneutics • Digital rhetoric

Apps as Closed Systems

Digital poetry on mobile platforms invokes particular technological constraints on electronic literature creation and consumption. A constraint of apps (software applications) on mobile devices is that they are closed technical systems, and this can be a particular challenge to creative

J. Naji, *Digital Poetry*, https://doi.org/10.1007/978-3-030-65962-2_4

practitioners such as digital poets who have often built on a more hacktiv-ist[1] approach to technological content creation. Unlike browser-based[2] content it is difficult to access app source code, and many of the technolo-gies required to create content for mobile devices are commercialised and proprietary as opposed to open source and shareable as can be found in browser-based options. Burgess (2012: 30) cites similar criticisms from Zittrain (2008) of iOS platforms, in particular, as hampering innovation and democracy because of their corporate enclosure of media technolo-gies, which removes access and agency from users by practices such as restricting access to source code. However, Burgess (2012: 40) takes a slightly different approach and argues that although iOS platforms lack "hackability" they can offer instead increased potential social and cultural "generativity" through the extra functionality offered by apps.

These problematics of form in creation and consumption are evident in the difficulty in even sourcing examples of digital poetry apps. For exam-ple, a frequent go to source for electronic literature is the Electronic Literature Organisation's collections, of which to date they have created three volumes.[3] The volumes are accessed through a browser so if one is to search for the keyword "mobile" some examples are found but in fact the user can only view the apps through video documentation. This is a similar challenge for VR platforms also, that require access to expensive commercially guarded technologies in order to access content. The seem-ingly closed and commercial environment of mobile platforms has led many digital poets away from them back to browser-based content with open source options that can offer less sophisticated aesthetics, but increased accessibility.

---

[1] Some digital art projects of which digital poetry could be considered a subset are hacktiv-ism oriented and seek to impact or comment on contemporary societal issues by repurposing existing technologies to a creative and artistic purpose. Strehovec (2008: 242) defines hack-tivism as a term that refers to civil disobedience activities of hackers and political activists who believe that "traditional society institutions are more vulnerable in their cyberspace forms than in their traditional representations bound to the physical world." Similarly, Amerika (2007: 402) discusses writing itself as hacktivism and suggests that digital writers need to reconfigure themselves as "network provocateurs" and mentions "activist art hackers who use the Web and other resources to create a kind of interventionist cybertheater" (Amerika 2007: 403).

[2] Browser-based content refers to digital content accessed through a web browser, most usually on stand-alone computers as opposed to apps on mobile platforms.

[3] As of 2020 when this book was written.

DIGITAL RHETORIC AND DIGITAL INTERPRETATION

How then do we develop a theory of interpretation or meaning making for mobile digital poetry? Eyman (2015: 93) cites Bitzer's (1968) conceptualisation of rhetoric as a meaning-making activity through the creation of a discourse, which changes reality through thought and action as opposed to the direct application of energy to objects. What is useful from Eyman's (2015: 93) working of this concept is that he notes that none of the rhetoric theories he discusses addressed the possibility of nonhuman agents becoming rhetorical actors. This is why Eyman (2015: 93) tells us that digital rhetoric needs to "take into account the complications of the affordances of digital practices including circulation, interaction, and the engagement of multiple symbol systems within rhetorical objects, and its methods need to explicitly engage those complications and affordances." It is clear that understanding poetic meaning making in digital systems needs to incorporate the complicated and dynamic interplay of multiple symbol systems. This is somewhat similar to Light et al.'s (2018) suggestion of a walk through method in order to critically analyse apps, similar in nature to the close reading of a text conducted in literary studies, a walk through approach however also incorporates the digital environment of operation of the app which should include its operating model and modes of governance. To consider the digital environment of operation we must, as per Eyman (2015), include all rhetorical actors, and this is why consideration of gesture, the haptic interaction engaged by the human interpreter also needs to be considered. Interpretation, as in traditional poetry, remains key to the mobile digital poetry experience and can be seen therefore to take place on the human and non-human side, which is why this chapter delves into hermeneutics to unpack these processes. Even so, Romele (2020: location 693) understands that methodologies of interpretation can seek too rigid a science of signs in order to account for the nuances and dynamic flows that we find in the digital medium, so this complexity is why a more fluid postmodern approach is often instead used. For example, Pressman (2014: 3) offers a digital modernism approach and makes the case for examining digital texts as literature that requires close reading within the tradition of literary history.

Romele (2020: location 616) however reminds us of the importance of language in the philosophy of technology, given technologies are always embedded in signs and symbols that mediate their understandings and uses. Digital technologies Romele (2020: location 639) tells us are hermeneutic technologies of a specific kind given their capacity to reduce the distance between objects and their representations. Digital technologies offer representations of the world that must be interpreted in order to access the world (Romele 2020: location 639). Romele suggests that one could argue for digital machines of interpretation without proper understanding (Romele 2020: location 3579). Capurro (2010: 35) reminds us of hermeneutics as a philosophy of interpretation of communication, which has fallen out of favour as a humanities methodology. Digital hermeneutics can help us to recognise the loss of the autonomy of the human interpreter in the human conversations mediated by digital technologies and that then questions the interpretational autonomy of human agents (Capurro 2010: 36). This is a key point given that it was already established through a posthuman lens that incorporation of non-human agents in the digital poetry experience is key to understanding how they work;[4] however we must now move one step further and recognise that in a similar way to how *technocentric* approaches to digital literature are criticised[5] so too must we question *humancentric* or *anthropocentric* approaches that assign all interpretive authority to the human agent. Is this then merely a technocentric approach that has gone too far? I would argue not, rather it is a recognition of the considerable interpretative potential that exists in mobile digital poetry for ALL actors and that crucially the human interpreter does not have autonomy in the interpretative process.

HAPTIC HERMENEUTICS AND GESTURAL MEANING MAKING IN DIGITAL POETRY

Notably many of the same aspects, problems, strengths, weaknesses of analogue literature can be also found to be at play in mobile digital poetry despite the challenging and sometimes limiting technical aspects of developing/writing for this medium. Yet there does seem to be something unique about poetry in this form, perhaps it is the haptic nature of interaction, the seeming ability to literally make things happen through touch that provides the reader with a potentially more intimate experience than in other platforms. This is ideal for the purposes of digital poetry as the more intuitive nature of these technologies mean that the spell of the piece need not be broken by the need for the reader to lift her head and look for

[4] See Chap. 3, "Instapoetics and the Literary Algorithm."
[5] See Strehovec (2020: Online) in Chap. 5, "Eco-writing and Drone: Digital Poetry During the Anthropocene."

the mouse; a simple hand movement will be enough to proceed within the piece and the tactile process of the analogue is recreated in the digital through the haptic screen. Frosh 2019: 156) tells of haptic engagement that technologically instantiates both bodily and emotional potential of "being moved" and the pertinence of this in relation to digital poetry seems worthy of note. For what else do we expect from poetry but to be moved, and there seems to be something particular about the gesture of touch in mobile media. As Hjorth (2011: 444) proposes when discussing mobile media, "it is the touch of the device, the intimacy of the object, that makes it so meaningful," the tactile process of the analogue is recreated in the digital through the haptic screen. Richardson and Hjorth (2019: 3) further note the intimate, tactile, social and playful nature of mobile interfaces and that the interpretation of the intimate and haptic effects of touchscreen media have become a significant area of media research.

Meaning Making and Embodied Interaction

Interpretation leads to meaning making which is clearly a social process, and social processes and technological artifacts are interrelated and intertwined (Hutchby 2001: 441), which is why the study of technological affordances such as haptic gestures can help us understand the changing shape of human meaning making. Embodied interaction builds on Hutchby's concepts of technological affordances from his 2001 paper "Technologies, Texts and Affordances" and is a human computer interaction (HCI) term that can help us analyse human meaning making and appreciate the contextual, fluid and collaborative nature of meaning making in the digital realm. Paul Dourish (2001) discusses *embodied interaction* as an approach from the field of human computer interaction that is based on the understanding that "users create and communicate meaning through their interaction with the system (and with each other, through the system)" (Dourish 2001: Online). We can see therefore that the gestural interaction of touch screen mobile devices is an embodied interaction that can situate the human interpreter in the digital poetry experience in a more integrated manner than a point and click interaction can.

Similarly, Pelard (2018) refers to *tactile digital poetry* on mobile devices and talks of how poets avail of the affordances of mobile devices such as touch, vibration and fingerprint passcodes to create a new type of poetic language and an unseen form of expressiveness (Pelard 2016: Online). Pelard (2016: 3) explains that on mobile devices digital poetry is mediated through an interface and a screen and this forces a reformulation of the relationship between the body and the screen. Tactile digital poetry on mobile devices is the result of an aesthetic gesture based on a polysemiotic regime of hypermediacy and interactivity which allows the poem to be created through the interaction of the body, the screen and the text as substantial allies in the meaning-making process (Pelard 2018: 3).[6]

Poetry apps can be hard to find; search in the app store and you will find apps that relate to poetry but not ones that are poetry. Most of the examples I have come across were, thanks to the networks, that I have formed by being a member of the Electronic Literature Organisation. This is how I came across *Abra!* by Amaranth Borsuk, Kate Durbin and Ian Hatcher (& You); it offers a playful approach as per Hjorth (2011) and describes itself as a poetry instrument/spellbook that responds to touch. It is a playful piece that allows you to modify the text on screen in a myriad of different ways through touch. You can select specific spells from the top of the screen such as mutate, graft, prune, erase and cadabra. The reader can modify the poem by selecting one of these "spells" and then touching the text with her finger. At the bottom of the screen there is a rainbow dial that you can use to navigate the poems in the *Abra* cycle. The strengths of this piece lie in the colourful aesthetics and enormous scope for reader interaction in the variety of spells and settings the reader can access to modify the text and even include her own. The reader can then share her own creation easily on Facebook and Twitter or simply save a photo. This potential social media connectivity in *Abra* (Borsuk et al. 2015) is an aspect of the work that draws on the affordances of the mobile medium, which thrives on and even demands at times a social media connection as per Burgess' (2012: 40) argument that re-increased social and cultural *generativity* through the expanded functionality of mobile apps. Unusually, the app doesn't include audio which given the playful nature of the work potentially could have added an extra dimension to the experience; however, without it the reader's focus is retained on the written words.

Jason Edwards Lewis and Bruno Nadeau's PoEMM (Poetry for Excitable [Mobile] Media) project is an example of digital poetry on a mobile device that maintains a strong focus not only on written words but also very evocative (sometimes overpowering even) audio. PoEMM is a series of eight mobile iOS apps that deal with themes of belonging, identity, youth and multiculturalism amongst others. The touchscreen interactivity of the apps uses the pinch and swipe gestures we have come to

---

[6] Pelard's (2018) work is in French and I have provided my own translation here.

associate with iOS technology. The pieces also allow for the creation of your own version as well as connecting with online social media such as Twitter. The PoEMM website describes the apps as "making sense of crazy talk & kid talk, the meanings of different shades of purple, the conundrums of being a Cherokee boy adopted by Anglos and raised in northern California mountain country, and the importance of calling a sundae a sundae." There are eight apps available entitled: *What They Speak When They Speak to Me, Buzz Aldrin Doesn't Know Any Better, The Great Migration, Smooth Second Bastard, No Choice About the Terminology, The Summer the Rattlesnakes Came, The World Was White, The World That Surrounds You Wants Your Death* (PoEMM).

To look at one of these apps, *The World Was White* (Lewis et al. 2015), the reader is initially presented with a pure white screen on launching the app, which remains that way until the reader touches the screen at which point text appears. If the reader maintains a finger press onscreen and swipes she hears audio, so this very immediate reaction to her touch evokes a strong engagement with the piece by providing a sense of agency for the reader and her body and mind become connected to the device and are integrated into the poetic process.

There are many, many, more examples of mobile electronic literature available for download on the App Store and Google Play and online although they can be challenging to find as when searching for poetry apps quite often what appears are apps about poetry rather than apps that are poetry. Generally they are not the examples I choose to study with students in my digital media content creation classes as I cannot provide a mobile device for each student to access the digital text on and I can't expect all students to be able to pay to download the apps either. As a result, freeware open source browser-based examples are the ones I show students as they have an added benefit of the option to reverse engineer them by looking at source code to see how they were made so that my students may learn approaches to digital creative content creation. This is part of the reason why in my opinion digital poetry apps can get over-looked. Despite these challenges of access and technological constraints in mobile platforms, the intuitive nature of the haptic gesture can offer a way to incorporate the human agent in the poetic experience through embod-ied interaction that draws on already meaningful gestural signs.

Mangen (2008: 404) reminds us that reading using digital technology is multi-sensory in that the act of reading is dependent on the fact that we are both body and mind. While Pelard (2018) speaks of the connection between body and screen Mangen (2008) talks of the connection between body and mind, while this has always been the case and technology has always been intricately connected to the way we read and write when it comes to digital technologies, particularly those that require haptic or gestural interaction, the connection between mind and body is magnified. Mangen (2008: 416) talks of *haptic perception* or *kinaesthetic sense modality*, which involves tactile perception through our skin and also our positional perception of our limbs and digits. Mangen (2008: 416) suggests that phenomenological immersion is dependent on the materiality of reading print pages and that reading from a screen is a more detached experience. Notably however Mangen (2008) uses electronic literature hypertext case studies to make this case and I would argue that in fact the type of phenomenological immersion and connection between body and mind in the reading process is possible in digital poetry on mobile devices when a more sophisticated interaction such as a haptic gesture is incorporated in the work in a meaningful manner. Clicking and scrolling are less intuitive interactions than pinch and swipe, and because clicking and scrolling are less intuitive, more jarring interactions, they can disjoint the immersive literary experience. Furthermore, the poetic experience can require less of a linear narrative than other literary forms and so is more suited to the playful nature or lusory sensibility of mobile devices that Richardson and Hjorth (2019) refer to. The hypertext fictions that Mangen (2008) discusses were created for a click and point interaction, Mangen (2008) is correct in that materiality matters, but so does the type of gesture required to interact with the computer and the closer that gesture or movement is to a potentially meaningful body movement then the less jarring it is to the literary immersion.

Cayley (2018: 3) speaks of the phenomenology of gesture too and tells us that gesture remains gesture until it is seized by what he terms *grammalepsy* and then it becomes a meaningful sign within the world of language. Therefore, the haptic gestures become objects of hermeneusis within the world of language. So the haptic gestures in a digital poem become subsumed into the poetic field of signs. Even though it is not a poem *Pry* (Gorman and Cannizzaro 2015) is a useful example here; *Pry*, a self-described app novella, was made by Tender Claws, an art collective and studio founded by Danny Cannizzaro and Samantha Gorman. This app tells the story of James, a demolition expert who has returned from the Gulf war (Pry n.d.). Part 1 of *Pry* (Gorman and Cannizzaro 2015) was released in 2014 and is available for both iOS and android mobile platforms. What is particularly engaging about Pry is the way the haptic

4 HAPTIC HERMENEUTICS AND POETRY APPS 51

gestures of tap, swipe and pinch are also imbued with meaning. The haptic gestures are not simply there as replacements of a mouse click, they are part of the storytelling experience. To see through the main character James' eyes, you spread and hold open your fingers, using a "reverse pinch" gesture similar to one that could be used to actually open someone's eyes. We are also offered the option to enter James' subconscious by pinching and holding closed again in a gesture similar to one that might be used to close something. Further association of the name of the app novella *Pry* meaning to peer in or pull apart further reinforces the hermeneutic potential of haptic gesture of the reverse pinch. This tactile illusion of the act of opening and closing someone's eyes automatically imbues the reader with a feeling of intimacy with the main character. Sight, internal, external and lack thereof is a theme of the piece with the reader even being required to move his/her finger across braille on the screen as the character reads aloud. The ability is provided in *Pry* (Gorman and Cannizzaro 2015) to switch between the video-based photo realistic mode of the conscious and the surreal text and images of the subconscious where we find text, telling the story simply and plainly but in a non-linear associative manner evocative of our internal recollections of people and events.

I have used Cayley's comments on gesture from *Grammalepsy* (2018) to refer to the gestures used to interact with *Pry;* however, in an email to me about this chapter Cayley clarified that when he discusses gesture such as sign language in *Grammalepsy* it is in reference to "gestures that themselves become language once they become readable." According to Cayley (2020) the gestures used to interact with *Pry* do not themselves become a part of the language of the text, they are gestures that "transact with the text expressively and add to its meaning, and they do give access to some of that language in a manner that is expressive in terms of allegory: prying open of eyes; pinching to close them, but they don't become a part of the language of the work." However I would argue that the gestures do become part of the language of the embodied performance of the text and in that sense become part of the sphere of meaning of signs of the text.

The storytelling narrative in *Pry* is not straightforward and the full sequence of events is constructed accretively, but this seems appropriate for such an inherently distracted platform as mobile device users will quite potentially dip in and out of content as they simultaneously perform many different tasks on their device. Despite this capacity for a fragmented reading experience the piece nonetheless still maintains a sense of momentum for the reader, a desire to reveal the full story, to find out what really happened, which is key for any good story electronic or analogue.

This chapter has only skimmed the surface of just a few mobile digital poems, and as the PoEMM (n.d.: Online) website suggests, mobile devices can offer a more intimate interaction experience for a reader and the higher resolution screen can provide an aesthetically pleasing visual and textual experience. Larissa Hjorth (2011: 440) refers to haptic screens in relation to the touch screens of mobile media and suggests that the screen is no longer about sight but about touch. It is interesting to note that it is the more "poetic" apps that seem to be more suited to the mobile medium as there is less of a sense of a beginning, middle and end to them. Poetry's non-reliance on linearity means that it is easier for a reader to dip in and out of each of these apps whereas when reading *Pry* (Gorman and Cannizzaro 2015), for example, a story, the reader is more likely to seek an end, a resolution as such, whereas when reading *The World Was White* (Lewis et al.) and *Abra* (Borsuk et al.) a reader is more likely to be open to a non-linear experiential and playful literary engagement.

Summary

This chapter sought to develop a theory of interpretation or meaning making for digital poetry on mobile platforms by recognising the unique nature of gesture required for interaction with haptic devices. This chapter built on discussions in Chap. 3, "Instapoetics and the Literary Algorithm," by not only further recognising the possibility of non-human agents becoming rhetorical actors within digital poetry interpretation but also crucially recognising the loss of autonomy of the human interpreter. Furthermore, this chapter situated the haptic gesture within a hermeneutic framework, which demonstrated how it can offer an embodied literary experience by linking in a meaningful way the mind/body connection more explicitly with the screen of the device.

References

Amerika, M. 2007. *Meta/Data: A Digital Poetics.* Cambridge, MA: MIT Press.
Borsuk, A., K. Durbin, and I. Hatcher. 2015. *Abra!.* Computer Software. Apple App Store. Vers. 1.0.
Burgess, J. 2012. Studying Mobile Media: Cultural Technologies, Mobile Communication, and the IPhone. In *Studying Mobile Media: Cultural*

Technologies, Mobile Communication, and the IPhone, ed. L. Hjorth, Burgess, J., and I. Richardson. London: Taylor & Francis Group. Accessed 15 September 2020, from ProQuest Ebook Central.

Capurro, R. 2010. Digital Hermeneutics: An Outline. *AI & Soc* 25: 35–42. https://doi.org/10.1007/s00146-009-0255-9.

Cayley, J. 2018. *Grammalepsy*. New York: Bloomsbury.

———. 2020. Email to Jeneen Naji, October 29.

Dourish, P. 2001. *Where the Action Is: The Foundations of Embodied Interaction*. Cambridge, MA: MIT Press.

Eyman, D. 2015. *Digital Rhetoric: Theory, Method, Practice*. Ann Arbor: University of Michigan Press. Accessed 15 September 2020. http://www.jstor.org/stable/j.ctv65swm2.

Frosh, P. 2019. *The Poetics of Digital Media*. Medford, MA: Polity.

Gorman, S., and D. Cannizzaro. 2015. *Pry*. Computer Software. Apple App Store. Vers. 1.1.0. Tender Claws LLC, 2014. Web. 30 November 2015.

Hjorth, L. 2011. Domesticating New Media: A Discussion on Locating Mobile Media. In *The New Media and Technocultures Reader*, ed. S. Giddings and M. Lister, 437–448. London and New York: Routledge. Print.

Hutchby, I. 2001. Technologies, Texts and Affordances. *Sociology* 35 (2): 441–456. https://doi.org/10.1177/S0038038501000219.

Lewis, J.E., S. Maheau, C. Gratton, and B. Nadeau. 2015. *The World Was White*. Computer Software. Apple App Store. Vers. 1.0.2. Jason Lewis. Web. 30 November 2015.

Light, B., J. Burgess, and S. Duguay. 2018. The Walkthrough Method: An Approach to the Study of Apps. *New Media & Society* 20 (3): 881–900. https://doi.org/10.1177/1461444816675438.

Mangen, A. 2008. Hypertext Fiction Reading: Haptics and Immersion. *Journal of Research in Reading* 31: 404–419. https://doi.org/10.1111/j.1467-9817.2008.00380.x.

Pelard, E. 2016. *How to Rethink Poetry with Mobile Devices and Touch Screens?* Abstract for DHBenelux Conference 2016, 9–10 June, Belval, Luxembourg. Accessed 15 September 2020. http://www.dhbenelux.org/wp-content/uploads/2016/05/90_Pelard_FinalAbstract_DHBenelux2016_short.pdf.

———. 2018. Poésies numériques tactiles : toucher les signes par la 'main de l'œil', manipuler la matière à l'écran. *Itinéraires [En ligne]*, 2017-3 | 2018, mis en ligne le 15 juin 2018, consulté le 01 mai 2019. http://journals.openedition.org/itineraires/3983; https://doi.org/10.4000/itineraires.3983.

PoEMM. n.d. Online. Accessed 15 September 2020. https://www.poemm.net/.

Pressman, J. 2014. *Digital Modernism*. Oxford: Oxford University Press.

Pry. n.d. Online. Accessed 15 September 2020. https://tenderclaws.com/pry.

Richardson, I., and L. Hjorth. 2019. Haptic Play: Rethinking Media Cultures and Practices. *Convergence* 25 (1): 3–5. https://doi.org/10.1177/135485651 8815275.

Romele, A. 2020. *Digital Hermeneutics.* New York: Routledge.

Strehovec, J. 2008. New Media Art as Research: Art-Making Beyond the Autonomy of Art and Aesthetics. *Technopoetic Arts: A Journal of Speculative Research* 6 (3): 233–250. https://doi.org/10.1386/tear.6.3.233/1.

———. 2020. Smart Technology Instead of Blood and Soil. *Electronic Book Review*, 5 July. Accessed 15 September 2020. https://doi.org/10.7273/3rjs-cl10.

Zittrain, J. 2008. *The Future of the Internet—And How to Stop It.* New Haven and London: Yale University Press.

CHAPTER 5

Eco-writing and Drone: Digital Poetry During the Anthropocene

Abstract This chapter examines eco-writing and digital methods of resistance that seek to highlight, combat and draw attention to ecological concerns. Drones, also known as remotely piloted aircraft (RPA), are primarily recognised as militaristic in function. However, we can see how technologies such as drones that were originally envisaged for military or commercial use have been quickly subsumed into a new art world of digital artistic practice and poetic expression such as drone poetry. In this chapter digital poems such as Richard A. Carter's (*Waveform*, 2017b) Waveform project, Shelly Jackson's *Snow* (2014–present) and Pip Thornton's 2016 {poem}. py are discussed from a position that examines the material ability of technologies to critique the very changes they are implicated in.

Keywords Drone poetry • Eco-writing • Anthropocene • Technopositivism • Digital resistance • RPA

Ecopoetry and Digital Methods of Resistance

In the editor's preface to *The Ecopoetry Anthology* Fisher-Wirth and Street (2013: location 727) tell how in recent decades the term ecopoetry has come into use, most notably since the 1990s, and that it stems from nature poetry, a genre that uses nature as its inspiration. Ecopoetry has fluid boundaries, no clear definition and is poetry that reflects the concerns of humanity's environmental crisis. It can suffer, they say, from hyperintellectualism and emotional detachment but there is poetic power and literary impact in a biocentric approach (Fisher-Wirth and Street 2013: location 762). Digital ecopoetry has even more fluid boundaries and a problematic ontology in that the technologies used in the creation of digital ecopoetry are strongly implicated in the processes that ecopoetry seeks to critique. For example, Richard Carter's *Waveform* project speaks very clearly to Crutzen and Stoermer's (2000) Anthropocene theory that posits that the Earth is entering a new geological epoch based on the sizable and fundamental impact of human activity on planet earth (Carter 2018a). As a practice-led researcher Richard's focus is on generating different methods through digital media technologies in order to investigate how the observable world is represented (Carter 2018a: 367). *Waveform* uses a drone platform to capture images of different wave patterns across Cornish beaches in the United Kingdom. These images collected by a drone were then processed using machine vision software that Carter developed himself using the open-source IDE (integrated development environment) *Processing*. This software would draw a line where it detected the shoreline to be and these data points were then used by an algorithm that Carter developed in *Processing* to generate poetry that was thematically responsive to the maritime aspects of the source imagery (Carter 2017a: Online). This project is a nod to the first computer poem created by Strachey on the Ferranti Mark I machine[1] and seeks to update Strachey's "original creative gesture for the task of meditating on the global sensory infrastructures that radar, algebraic signal processing, and digital computing gave rise to" (Carter 2018a: 371). Carter (2018b, Online) states that *Waveform* uses technology that is implicated in the geopolitical-capitalist struggles of past decades and seeks to interrogate normative representations made of the world using digital sensors.

Carter's *Waveform* project could be seen as an example of Amanda Starling Gould's (2016) suggested approach to counteracting the absence of environmental thinking from both digital theory and popular digital rhetoric (2016: 1). Gould (2016: 1) proposes "a *digital environmental media studies* (DEMS) framework that shifts the primary focus of digital media study from one grounded in computation to one fully rooted in the earth." In her 2016 paper "Restor(y)ing the Ground: Digital Environmental Media Studies" Gould gives the example of then President Obama's 2015 selfie on Instagram that attempted to draw attention to the impact of

[1] See Chap. 2, "What Is Digital Poetry?"

climate change. And yet, Gould (2016: 1) tells us that in the ensuing vibrant debate online it was omitted that "the very devices and networked connections required to use the mobile-only Instagram platform are among the most noxious of modern contributors to climate change."

This corresponds to Streheovec's (2020: Online) critiques of electronic literature academics and practitioners for overt technocentrism that is, in his opinion, too focused on the future promises of technology rather adopting a critical approach to the impact of technologies on the future of humanity. He cites new media art and hacktivism movements and methods of resistance that engage more readily with civil society and that media art forgoes a focus on aesthetics and situates itself beyond a technopositivist ideology (Strehovec 2020: Online). Is there a way then, that digital poetry can tackle environmental issues without becoming part of the problem?

DIGITAL METHODS OF RESISTANCE TO TECHNOCENTRISM

Poetry has a long history of resistance, perhaps more usually referred to as political poetry, and it can have a very real impact on politics itself. Boland (1995, Online) tells Cicero's "Pro Archia Poeta," "For Archias the Poet," the first written defence of political poetry. Poetry was also an important part of the Irish nationalist movement in the nineteenth century with most notably the publication of "the Spirit of the Nation" a pamphlet of poetry which advocated a return to Irish language and a new self-reliance and it proved to be more popular than the local paper in some towns (Boland 1995, Online). Plys (2020) discusses resistance poetry during India's emergency in 1975 and argues that it helped form bonds and solidarity in resistance groups by "linking anti-state movements to the centuries-old tradition of Islamicate poetry, thereby fostering solidarity and providing a firm basis for collective action" (Plys 2020: 4). Similarly Kalra and Butt (2019: 1038) talk of resistance in Pakistan during General Zia's (1977–1988) political strategies and that during that period poetry in particular was a vehicle to "express discontent as well as to mobilize the population." And Kassis (2015) discusses Palestinian Samih al-Qasims' resistance poetry. The examples of political and resistance poetry are too many to list here but are important to note within the context of discussions in this chapter regarding digital poetry and methods of resistance because we can see that digital ecopoetry is building on a history of poetic resistance. However, what is unique about digital ecopoetry is that it is made from the very thing it is resisting. Technocentric discussions of the cyborg and digital literature and the lessening of boundaries between human and machine often omit mention of the impact of the cumulative effect on our bodies from "technology-related toxins and environmental habitat destruction" (Gould 2016: 8). Gould (2016: 8) suggests as a way forward rather than focus on the technocentric concept of the cyborgian body and instead to focus on the bodies that are doing the mining for the elements required for the construction of our ubiquitous digital devices. Telling the stories (Gould 2016: 9) suggests of the mine laborers; men, women and children in toxic work condition "reveals the marginalized bodies that are hidden by our fetishistic fascination with the digital's magical, Cloud-based immateriality."

Shelly Jackson tells an ecostory through her Instagram account *Snow* (2014–present) which is described by herself as "a story in progress, weather permitting"; however, it is poetic in form as each image posted is of one word written in snow and designed to be read backwards. Benzon (2019: 70) views Jackson's work as experimental electronic literature that interrogates "its own status as digital writing in order to consider the eco-politics of digital technology from the microscopic scale of the word, the typographic character, and the byte, to the macroscopic scale of global media and planetary climate." Jackson uses snow and slush of her outside living environments to write one word and take a photo of it in order to post it to her Instagram account @snowshelleyjackson. Benzon (2019: 71) suggests that "*Snow* exemplifies an emergent moment of critically and self-critically engaged digital literary production that provides an urgently needed response to the wide-ranging social and political implications of global computing." This however leads us to ask the question as to how can digital technologies that are implicated in the global changes being critiqued in the artwork be used legitimately to create that critique?

Using technologies that are implicated in processes that a poet is specifically critiquing, in the manner suggested by Gould (2016) and Strehovec (2020), can be particularly effective as long as the creation process is thoughtful about not contributing in a material manner to the problem that is being critiqued. Pip Thornton takes this approach in her self-described piece of "political art" entitled {poem}.py (2016) as part of her 2019 PhD thesis on *Language in the Age of Algorithmic Reproduction* in which she ran a poem through the Google AdWords keyword planner in order to represent the process of what she terms linguistic capitalism. In collaboration with her colleagues Ben Curtis and Giovanni Cherubin,

Thornton incorporated Python code that processed and gathered further data, which could then reorder the text into a poem receipt which was printed out through a second-hand receipt printer which she purchased on eBay (Thornton 2019: 174). The Google ads keyword planner is an advertising tool that suggests bid prices for ads and keywords that can be used in a Google keyword advertising campaign; some words are more expensive than others. Thornton discusses putting William Wordsworth's *Daffodils* through *[poem].py* and finding, for example, that the word "cloud" was more expensive than others because of the market value of cloud computing. Thornton (2019: 174) tells of her intention with *[poem].py* being to work from inside the technology without contributing to the marketplace. So Thornton used the tools and techniques of capitalism with bids and receipts without actually having to pay for anything and therefore contributed to the marketplace. Furthermore she highlights a specific difference of *[poem].py* from other "digital-art" projects: the final output of her piece is analogue, with a printed out poem receipt that lists the word and keyword prices of the words in the text that were put through the python code (Thornton 2019: 176).

It is clear that digital technologies are so embedded in our daily lives and integrated in all aspect of humanities communicative and knowledge building practices that the suggested approach of not using digital technologies at all is not plausibly put forward as a method of resistance to ecological concerns. Or perhaps it is but we just don't hear about it because those who do it are not online. Paradoxically digital technologies can also help communicate the implications of the impact of ecological concerns. Ledesma (2018: location 235) refers to "online activist eco-poetry" as a valuable tool in the dynamics of grass-roots resistance in Brazil. In it he gives examples of indigenous communities' online poetry publications in Brazil on a variety of formats such as Twitter and blogs thereby making them visible to a global audience, which can then help "apply pressure to a slow-to-move political class" (Ledesma 2018: location 5796). This use of digital tools in resistance campaigns by indigenous communities is similar to how the Native American NO DAPL movement incorporated drone technology into their overall strategy of protest alongside intense media activity that used social networks as well as traditional ritual activities and camera drones and live streaming (Martini 2018: 44–45). Michele Martini (2018: 45) cites Kyriakidou (2015) to observe that in the context of social struggles drone videos overcome their informational value and acquire an experiential and transformational one.

Whilst digital abstinence is not a popular method of resistance, slow computing is another approach that is gaining increasing popularity as a form of resistance in the algorithmic age; this method does not specifically speak to ecological concerns but rather by tracing new routes and directions that aim to embrace technology but not in a blithe uncritical manner (Fraser and Kitchin 2017: 1). Hacking and creative repurposing are one of the methods of slow computing and networked communities resistance to the commercially motivated proprietary technologies of today's digital technologies. As outlined in the history of digital poetry in Chap. 2, "What Is Digital Poetry?", digital poetry has a long history of engaging with such practices and Richard Carter's drone poetry could be seen as an example of this type of approach in which technology that is implicated in contemporary world changing practices can be used in a critical manner to highlight concerns or to force audiences to think about their own practice and think about potential alternatives for humanity's technocentric future.

Drone Poetry

In the 2015 book *A Theory of the Drone*, Grégoire Chamayou and Janet Lloyd quote 1930s philosopher Simone Weil who tells us to:

> *Go and look at the weapons, study their specific characteristics. Become a technician, in a way. But only in a way, for the aim here is an understanding that is not so much technical as political. What is important is not so much to grasp how the actual device works but rather to discover the implications of how it works for the action that it implements.* (Chamayou and Lloyd 2015: 15)

Chamayou and Lloyd reference Weil's work in relation to his overall aims in theorising drone technology within a very specific military weaponised use, but we can also see how it applies to other uses of drone technology. What about cultural and artistic uses such as poetry?

Martini (2018) discusses drone videos and draws on Chamayou and Lloyd's (2015) work within the context of media-based resistance strategies; he suggests that in a drone video, the point of view of the filming user and that of the watching user overlap in a third position which does not belong to either of them. What they both assume is a strictly non-human perspective, the perspective of a camera separated from the body of the camera operator which echoes Haraway's (1988: 581) "god-trick" the all-knowing, all seeing gaze facilitated by new technologies.[2] Drones operate on a delicate balance between "physical distance and ocular proximity" which regulates the intensity of the bond of intimacy linking events, filming-users and watching users (Chamayou and Lloyd 2015: 117). As Col. Chris Chambliss (US Military Drones Wing) states, "the emergence of such a bond of intimacy might be problematic for drone pilots" (Martini 2018: 44). Although the bond of intimacy has proven problematic for the human part of the drone killing and destroying machine, could that not be exploited for artistic forms of expression such as poetry in which intimacy is sought to be created? However, drone poetics, as Brady (2016: 123) quite rightly asserts, must extend beyond a mostly Western artistic position of individuals with a quality of life that is privileged enough to engage in cultural production.

The intimacy that Chamayou and Lloyd refer to that drone operators develop is created through operators shadowing their targets for weeks (Chamayou and Lloyd 2015: 117), although mediated by an interface it is a visual intimacy formed through familiarity with the victims. The perceived lack of agency in killings by the human operator through the use of a drone could be discounted by evidence of cases of PTSD exhibited by drone operators (Chappelle et al. 2014: 480). The drone and operating agent are implicated in contemporary geo and socio-political processes to a high degree. This is why Carter (2017b) uses drone technology in his *Waveform* project as the militaristic innovation is implicated deeply in the very changes it is observing.

In 2013 David Shook ran a Kickstarter campaign to raise funds to create a "Poetry Drone" that "re-appropriates the unmanned aerial vehicle to deploy poems addressing the US military's use of drones" (Shook 2013: Online). The campaign was ultimately unsuccessful, but it is clear that drone poetry is not as niche an area as we may at first think it is. Google the phrase "drone poetry" and not only will you find listings for text-based poems about drones, but you will also find YouTube videos of footage shot from drones with poetic voice overs and text superimposed. Andrea Brady (2016: 119) tells of artistic movements like "New Aesthetic" that consider drones as potential inspiration for new artistic practices. Most artworks that use drone technology are visual, Brady (2016: 120) tells us, and she gives examples of some as well as many textual and lyrical

---

[2] I discuss this in more detail in Chap. 6, "Poetic Mirror Worlds and Mixed Reality Poetry," with reference to embodied interaction in VR.

engagements. This chapter is however concerned with poetry made using drone technology rather than written about drone technology.

Brady (2016: 116) tells of how there is a proliferation of drone artworks and poems but notes that although these artworks critique drone operations they are not concerned with the "phenomenological implications of executions from the air". Contemporary technologies such as drones and VR provide a top-down omnipresent view that gives us the sense that we are omnipresent beings in control of our environment in a relationship of domination (Brady 2016: 135). This once more reminds us of Haraway's (1988: 581) "god trick" and Brady (2016: 116) proposes *Drone Poetics* that include: "the objectification of the target, the domination of visuality, psychic and operational splitting, the 'everywhere war', the intimacy of keyhole observations, and the mythic or psychoanalytic representation of desire and fear." These six implications, Brady (2016: 116) concludes, indicate the need for a revision of our thinking regarding the practice of writing poetry in the drone age. Given the non-human position of the camera which is separated from its operator I suggest building on this one step further and recognising that in the posthuman age we inhabit, non-human socio-technical inventions have had dramatic impact on our environment, relationships, communications and as a result cultural production such as poetry. Therefore it is not only drone poetry that demonstrates the need to update our understandings of modern writing but in fact all of our contemporary cultural production and the distilled nature of the poetic form can provide us with a useful object through which we can analyse these changes. I will develop these thoughts further in the conclusion of this book.

SUMMARY

This chapter has sought to question technocentric approaches to digital poetry and has critically questioned the use of digital tools and technologies in examples of digital eco-writing that look to highlight ecological concerns. In doing so it has shown how digital poetry has continued to draw on historical methods of poetic resistance to tackle societal and environmental concerns. Drone poetry in particular was seen to emerge as a type of digital poetry that highlights the need to recognise changes in writing practices in a technologised age and the ethical implications of such. Gould's *Digital Environmental Media Studies* (2016) and Brady's (2016) *Drone Poetics* emerged as key frameworks that could be used to critically examine drone poetry towards the goal of a recognition of more complex and technologised ways of writing that offers approaches that can potentially incorporate contemporary societal considerations.

REFERENCES

Benzon, P. 2019. Weather Permitting: Shelley Jackson's Snow and the Ecopoetics of the Digital. *College Literature* 46 (1): 67–95.
Boland, E. 1995. Writing the Political Poem in Ireland. *Southern Review* 31(3): 485. Accessed 13 August 2020. https://search-ebscohost-com.jproxy.nuim. ie/login.aspx?direct=true&db=a9h&AN=9508243312&site=ehost-live.
Brady, A. 2016. Drone Poetics. *New Formations* 89: 116–136.
Carter, R. 2017a. Drone Poetry—On Deploying Sensory Technologies as Tools of Writing. *The Writing Platform*. Accessed 13 June 2019. http://thewritingplat-form.com/2017/09/drone-poetry-deploying-sensory-technologies-tools-writing/.
———. 2017b. *Waveform*. Accessed 21 September 2020. http://richardacarter. com/waveform/.
———. 2018a. Airborne Inscription: Writing with Drones. *EVA Copenhagen 2018—Politics of the Machines—Art and After*. https://doi.org/10.14236/ ewic/EVA2018.69.
———. 2018b. Waves to Waveforms: Performing the Thresholds of Sensors and Sense-Making in the Anthropocene. *Arts* 7 (4): 70, 15. https://www.mdpi. com/2076-0752/7/4/70.
Chamayou, G., and J. Lloyd. 2015. *A Theory of the Drone*. New York: The New Press.
Chappelle, W., T. Goodman, L. Reardon, and W. Thompson. 2014. An Analysis of Post-traumatic Stress Symptoms in United States Air Force Drone Operators. *Journal of Anxiety Disorders* 28 (5): 480–487.
Crutzen, P., and E. Stoermer. 2000. The Anthropocene. *IGBP Global Change* 41: 17–18.
Fisher-Wirth, A., and L. Street, eds. 2013. *The Ecopoetry Anthology*. San Antonio, TX: Trinity University Press. Accessed 16 August 2020. http://www.amazon. co.uk/kindlestore.
Fraser, A., and R. Kitchin. 2017. *Slow Computing*, SocArXiv, 6 December. https:// doi.org/10.31235/osf.io/rmxfk.
Gould, A. 2016. Restor(y)ing the Ground: Digital Environmental Media Studies. *Networking Knowledge: Journal of the MeCCSA Postgraduate Network* 9 (5): 1–19.

Haraway, D. 1988. Situated Knowledges: The Science Question in Feminism and the Privilege of Partial Perspective. *Feminist Studies* 14(3): 575–599. Published by: Feminist Studies, Inc. http://www.jstor.org/stable/3178066.

Jackson, S. 2014–present. *Snow.* Instagram. Accessed 21 September 2020. https://www.instagram.com/snowshelleyjackson/?hl=en.

Kalra, V., and W. Butt. 2019. 'If I Speak, They Will Kill Me, to Remain Silent Is to Die': Poetry of Resistance in General Zia's Pakistan (1977–88). *Modern Asian Studies* 53 (4): 1038–1065.

Kassis, S. 2015. Samih al-Qasim: Equal Parts Poetry and Resistance. *Journal of Palestine Studies* 44(2): 43–51. Published by University of California Press on Behalf of the Institute for Palestine Studies Stable. https://www.jstor.org/stable/10.1525/jps.2015.44.2.43.

Kyriakidou, M. 2015. Media Witnessing: Exploring the Audience of Distant Suffering. *Media Culture & Society* 37 (2): 215–231.

Ledesma, E. 2018. Online Activist Eco-Poetry: Techno-Cannibalism, Digital Indigeneity, and Ecological Resistance in Brazil. In *Online Activism in Latin America,* ed. H. Chacón (Routledge Studies in New Media and Cyberculture) Format: Kindle Edition New York: Routledge.

Martini, M. 2018. On the User's Side: YouTube and Distant Witnessing in the Age of Technology-Enhanced Mediability. *Convergence* 24 (1): 33–49. https://doi.org/10.1177/1354856517736980.

Plys, K. 2020. The Poetry of Resistance: Poetry as Solidarity in Postcolonial Anti-Authoritarian Movements in Islamicate South Asia. *Theory, Culture & Society.* https://doi.org/10.1177/0263276419882735.

Shook, D. 2013, *The Poetry Drone.* Accessed 21 September 2020. https://www.kickstarter.com/projects/shookshookshook/the-poetry-drone.

Strehovec, J. 2020. Smart Technology Instead of Blood and Soil. *Electronic Book Review,* July 5. Accessed 15 September 2020. 10.7273/3rjs-c110.

Thornton, P. 2016. *{poem}.py.* Accessed 21 September 2020. https://pipthornton.com/2016/06/12/poem-py-a-critique-of-linguistic-capitalism/.

———. 2019. *A Critique of Linguistic Capitalism.* PhD Thesis, Royal Holloway, University of London.

CHAPTER 6

Poetic Mirror Worlds and Mixed Reality Poetry

Abstract This chapter describes examples of mixed reality (MR) poetry which spans a continuum from virtual reality (VR) to augmented reality (AR). There is clearly identifiable digital poetry being created in MR platforms such as Borsuk and Bouse's *Between Page and Screen* (2016). However, MR works such as Laurie Anderson and Hsin-Chien Huang's *Chalkroom* (2017) and Mez Breeze and Andy Campbell's *All the Delicate Duplicates* (2017) are harder to define. These are projects that incorporate considerable use of poetic text so an argument could be made to categorise them as MR poetry; however, they could also be categorised as experiential games. This chapter uses these examples of mixed reality poetry as case studies in which to examine the changing role of words in virtual spaces.

Keywords Mirror worlds • Virtual reality • Mixed reality • Virtual words • Text

Although digital poetry has yet to be fully recognised globally in order that it be included in traditional cannons, it is an existing and recognised genre of which mixed reality poetry is an even newer emerging subset. I will firstly explain what mixed reality is before outlining some examples of mixed reality poetry within the context of a discussion regarding the changing modalities of virtual words in human places. The selection of

J. Naji, *Digital Poetry*, https://doi.org/10.1007/978-3-030-65962-2_6

mixed reality poetry that I offer is by no means exhaustive and I have selected them purely based on my own selfish interests as one would pick up a particularly attractive shell on a beach walk. It isn't possible for me to document each shell, or in this case each type of mixed reality poetry in existence, but that isn't to say that we cannot gain some knowledge and insight by examining a select few examples.

What Is Mixed Reality?

Mixed reality (MR) is best understood within the context of a reality-virtuality continuum, which spans from the real environment to augmented reality (AR) and virtual reality (VR) (Milgram et al. 1995). VR is a computer-generated interactive experience in which the user wears a head-mounted display and immerses themselves completely in an entirely virtual three-dimensional (3D) digital world; the Oculus Rift is an example of this. For AR, the user can also wear a head-mounted display, but they see 3D objects superimposed on the real world; Microsoft's HoloLens is an example of AR technology. While VR allows a user to explore and be completely immersed in a 3D virtual environment, AR incorporates 3D digital objects within the world around you, this can be done using your mobile phone or a head-mounted display.

Mixed Reality Modalities and Multimodality

We commonly refer to "the language of film," or "the language of art," and soon we will be referring to the language of MR or VR. Naji et al. (2019: 150) outline how theories of multimodality have to date offered us an expanded approach to meaning making that takes into consideration multiple dimensions of representation such as graphics, video, audio, animation, text, speech and design and so on. It is common to come across examples of all these devices in digital media content and digital poetry generally, however now the move to immersive computing technologies has added even more dimensions to multimodality.

Humanity's technological transformations have resulted in the screen becoming the dominant site of representation and communication instead of the page, now the logic of the image dominates the semiotic organisation of the screen (Kress 2003: 65). What we see is reverse ekphrasis. This means that the visual is becoming the primary means of communication and words the secondary, instead of ekphrasis, where the words are the primary and the visual the secondary (Naji et al. 2019: 169). For example, in the majority of digital poetry the user is nearly always presented with visuals before they are presented with text. This is quite a dramatic change from poetry in print when the reader is always presented with text first. Or even for the listener as they also hear the words first before visualising the imagery. One exception however is concrete poetry whereby the reader is first presented with a visual image or shape before reading the words. These theories clearly now need to be updated for mixed reality poetry in immersive media as we now have to incorporate spatial and gestural dimensions in humanity's technological transformation away from the screen into virtual space. Murray (2017: 184) suggests that, given the expanded space dimensionality in virtual environments movement can now be used as a social language. Given the potentially expanded modes of meaning now apparent in virtual spaces, it is important to think about what transformations have taken place in relation specifically to the semiotic unit that is a word.

Virtual Words and Mixed Reality Poetry

Strehovec (2010: 71) tells us that in "the digital medium, the word loses its authority and solidity—which characterized its role in printed texts—and it appears as the raw material for numerous transformations and interventions." Strehovec (2010: 82) discusses digital poetry by placing it within the broader field of new media art and interface culture. He posits that we "bear witness to the birth of a highly visualized, malleable, and flexible word, incorporated into the film of verbal messages" (Strehovec 2010: 63). It is clear therefore that text in the digital age does not hold the same power as it does in print. Nonetheless despite this, text in a sense is always present in the digital realm in that it is always present visually and/ or aurally or even as code. Simanowski (2010: 162) tells us that it is the materiality of text in digital media that is focused on which can often undermine its linguistic signification. A focus instead on words as opposed to text is more useful to digital poetry critical analysis as words can be an important identifying feature in poetry. The essentiality and importance of words continue in mixed reality poetry where they continue to act not only as semiotic objects but also as affordances, as we are about to discuss.

The Electronic Literature Organisation (Online n.d.-a) states that the "field of electronic literature is an evolving one. Literature today not only migrates from print to electronic media; increasingly, *born digital* works are created explicitly for the networked computer." The term not only refers to pieces of literature created solely in and experienced through the computer but also those works that began in print before moving to the digital. Noah Wardrip-Fruin defines digital literature as "a term for work with important literary aspects that requires the use of digital computation" (Funkhouser 2012: 3). Defining the boundary lines between digital genres is not an easy task, and while some texts are easily identified as mixed reality digital poetry such as *Between Page and Screen* (Borsuk and Bouse 2016) other game like VR works that incorporate the use of text such as Laurie Anderson and Hsin-Chien Huang's 2017 *Chalkroom* and Mez Breeze and Andy Campbell's 2017 *All the Delicate Duplicates* are harder to define.

Although initially popular as topic in the 1990s virtual reality has enjoyed a resurgence in the last decade as the technology is now more affordable and accessible than ever before, for example, the Oculus Rift. The Oculus Rift is head-mounted virtual reality technology that was developed by Oculus VR. As a researcher, I have experience with Cave technology, which has been around long before the Oculus Rift, and is an immersive, shared virtual reality environment created using goggles and several pairs of projectors, each pair pointing to the wall of a small room. The first Cave was developed at the University of Illinois at Chicago, which has trademarked the acronym Cave Automatic Virtual Environment (CAVE); some similar virtual environments are referred to with the term "cave," not used as an acronym (ELO, Online n.d.-b). Works of electronic literature have been made for a cave, most notably at Brown University where I was lucky enough to research as a Fulbright TechImpact Scholar in 2014. What is interesting in the case of Brown University is that although the Cave technology was initially developed and housed by science departments, such as Computer Science and Applied Mathematics, it has since been used in the department of Literary Arts for digital writing.

The Rubayaat

The Rubayaat is a mixed reality poem that I created with the Cave in Brown University in order to explore notions of translation, multiculturalism and the impact of technological affordances on literary expression and reception. This was done through creating a digital version of the poem *The Rubáiyát of Omar Khayyám* (Fitzgerald 1993) one that allows the user to experience, simultaneously, different translations of this work in

English, Irish, Arabic and Farsi. This provides the reader with an opportunity to simultaneously access, in the virtual space, alternative versions of the text, some of which may fall outside the mainstream. For example, the digital Cave version includes not only the well-known English language translation by Edward Fitzgerald from the nineteenth century but also a lesser known 1899 (Nash Cadell) English language version *The Rubáiyát of Omar Khayyám* by Mrs. Henry Moubray Cadell (née Jessie E. Nash), a nineteenth-century Persian scholar who dedicated her life to this translation and the study of the Persian language. The Arabic translation of the poem by the twentieth-century Egyptian poet Ahmed Rami is also included as distorted audio sung by Oumm Khalthoum, a twentieth-century Egyptian singer, accompanied by the original text in Farsi from the eleventh and twelfth centuries, in addition to an Irish language version intended to represent the research-author's multicultural identity. The user steps into the cube space of the Cave and by using goggles and a remote control navigates the immersive VR environment however they please. The piece uses multilingual kinetic text and audio, and the user navigates the virtual reality space through movement and a remote control, whilst wearing specific 3D glasses that the computer uses to track the user's position in the virtual space. The user can zoom into words until they tower above them or zoom out to be seen from a distance; this functionality has the ability to change profoundly our relationship to text and words as virtual words develop an entirely new power.

In mixed reality examples such as *The Rubayaat* it is clear that words behave very differently than we are used to in print. This is why it is important to consider what happens to the word in mixed reality spaces, text can become a visual sculptural object in an environment that integrates multiple communication modalities in real-time. As such, though text might not hold the same power as it does in print, words do, although the word as we know it has died, it has instead been transformed into a more multi-modal object. This is similar to John Cayley's prediction in 2006, that as three-dimensional immersive representations become more prevalent as technology develops, language can and will have a role to play in VR; however, ultimately this will be mediated. Symbolic and literal materiality will not only exist in our virtual spaces, it can contribute to their very constitution, to shape and define these spaces (Cayley 2006: 14). Furthermore, given the expanded space dimensionality in virtual environments movement can now be used as a social language (Murray 2017: 184). In fact, Janet Murray proposes that for genres beyond narrative, we can identify four affordances—the procedural, the participatory, the encyclopaedic and the spatial—that together support new forms of interactivity and immersion (Lashley and Creech 2017: 1078).

Mixed reality spaces offer immersive environments that integrate multiple communication modalities and affordances such as those outlined by Murray (Lashley and Creech 2017: 1078). By providing real-time sensory stimulation across multiple modalities, VR can immerse the user in a simulated reality, as opposed to viewing one from the outside in. This forces us to ask what impact do immersive digital environments have on hermeneutics most specifically in relation to words? To look at, for example, contemporary screen-based Instagram poetry which is discussed in Chap. 3, "Instapoetics and the Literary Algorithm," the poetic words become part of the image, subsumed and cannibalised into a primarily visual semiotic framework. In these instances, it is the words that we traditionally identify as poetry, it is the words that differentiate these Instagram posts from others to make them identifiable as poetry and yet it is the words that get subsumed into what Kress (2003: 7) terms the logic of the image. In VR text can become a visual sculptural object in an environment that integrates multiple communication modalities in real-time such as in the next example of mixed reality poetry.

Chalkroom

In an interview with Laurie Anderson in 2018, Bonnie Marranca comments on *Chalkroom* (Anderson and Huang 2017) that although it is a VR piece, it in fact uses the oldest of forms, writing and drawing. *Chalkroom* is a VR collaboration between Laurie Anderson and Hsin-Chien Huang, which won the Best Virtual Reality Experience award at the *74th Venice International Film Festival* in 2017. You could argue that winning an award at a film festival makes it a film but *Chalkroom* is a striking VR piece in that everything is made from words and letters. There are drawings that look like they have been written by hand with chalk and you navigate through a dark environment in which the writing and drawings glow white. As you explore the VR environment you hear Anderson's voice and it is an experiential process in which you can encounter stories told through visual words and pictures and audio. Anderson explains that she didn't like the visual language of VR because it is so oriented to gaming structures so she and her collaborator, Hsin-Chien Huang, invented this other way of doing it that is a more atmospheric visual language (Anderson and

Marranca 2018). It is a perfect example to discuss here in that its very clear and explicit use of text makes it easy to classify as digital literature whereas quite often most VR pieces are more usually considered games as they can be task oriented and use the visual language of games whereas this is very clearly a storytelling experience that draws heavily on the semiotic field of the written word but also as a sculptural object.

Text and words as sculptural objects are a concept worth exploring in an age of VR, and Wilsher (2019) argues that a phenomenological link to the disembodied experience in VR should be explored. In order to do this Wilsher (2019: 14) suggests that historical theories of sculpture may be helpful because they help us understand the role of the human body in the perception of sculpture. Wilsher (2019: 14) quotes VR artist Rachel Rossin who said that in VR it is only the memory of a body that is invoked. He also quotes Anderson who similarly, with reference to *Chalkroom* (Anderson and Huang: 2017), talks of how her works have always dealt with themes of "bodilessness" and that in fact she approaches it from a space of freedom to be totally absorbed in a technologically mediated universe (Wilsher 2019: 14). But Wilsher (2019: 13) asks is this not just another version of what Haraway (1988: 581) critiques as the god trick, seeing everything from nowhere? Haraway argues that a new language of embodiment for 3D technologies is needed that recalls and considers the presence of body. He invokes Haraway's suggested response to the "god-trick" is "situated knowledge" which recognises and values the corporeal subject position (Wilsher 2019: 13). The importance of remembering the existence of the body in mixed reality spaces, even when the intention is to leave the body behind, is an important point that we will return to.

All the Delicate Duplicates

All the Delicate Duplicates (Breeze and Campbell 2017) describes itself as a work of fiction, that constructs a storyworld through a PC game and a web-based short story. What is interesting about *All the Delicate Duplicates* (Breeze and Campbell 2017) is not only the fact that text is an important semiotic and gameplay element in the work but also that it identifies itself as fiction. O'Sullivan (2019: location 1667) describes *All the Delicate Duplicates* (Breeze and Campbell 2017) as an inherently literary work and as electronic literature but also as a literary game as evidenced by its availability on Steam a gaming platform.

To continue the discussion regarding virtual words *All the Delicate Duplicates* is a notable example because it uses *Mezangelle* a digitally born language that constructs poetic phrases to extend and enhance meaning beyond the expected (Breeze 2018: 1). Breeze (2018: 10), one of the authors of *All the Delicate Duplicates*, explains that *Mezangelle* remixes the English language and code to create a new language with nested meanings that can be unpacked with multiple readings in order to construct a narrative.

Cramer (2002: Online) describes *Mezangelle* as a rich semantical private language that is itself a play on the author's name Mez Breeze that draws on ASCII Art and Net.art code. Breeze (2018: 8) has used *Mezangelle* in other works and tells us that meaning in *Mezangelle* is dependent on an acknowledgment that there are many possibilities for a "correct" answer. Mezangelle promotes multiple pathways and meanings which are demonstrated in the ways that the backstory for *All the Delicate Duplicates* (2017) is constructed.

Strehovec (2017: Online) discusses text-based digital installations such as *All the Delicate Duplicates* (Breeze and Campbell 2017) that require specialist technology and defines them as a key modality of digital literature. Strehovec cites Simon Biggs' *Tower* which when explored in VR "spoken words appear to float and join a spiralling history of previously spoken words. As an uttered word emerges, other words, predicted on the basis of statistical frequency within a textual corpus, spring up. We encounter spoken words as well as those suggested by algorithms. The number of spiral word structures constantly increases" (Strehovec 2017: Online).

Strehovec notes the vanishing and abstract use of text in digital literature projects, and based on the examples discussed in this chapter that does seem to be the case. Legibility of text does not seem to be a priority and text is incorporated in quite a poetic, abstract, atmospheric and experiential manner open to interpretation rather than requiring users to read each word in sequence. This type of conditional legibility of text Strehovec (2017) sees as part of poetry's resistance to the language of mainstream capitalism in direct opposition to the more literal graphic sophistication and social interactions and interventions of other installations. The expanded and transformed potentialities of meaning of text in the virtual space serve to highlight the enormous impact that virtual space has had on human thought and meaning making. It is clear that these virtual spaces are increasingly becoming of equal, if not more, importance to our analogue spaces and the concept of mirror worlds is useful here to begin to unpack the matter of our increasingly important and expanding virtual twin worlds.

SPACE AND PLACE IN MIRROR WORLDS

In mixed reality digital poetry space and place are important, though we may find ourselves lost in virtual space we are still very much rooted in our bodies in a place. Ryan et al. (2016: 6) note that the science and humanities use the terms of space, place and "sense of place" in a number of ways. These terms are central to the work of geographers but also to writers and virtual reality developers. In 2015, narrative theorist Marie-Laure Ryan alludes to the human geographer Yi-Fu Tuan's celebrated concepts of both space and place as contrasting entities. Ryan explains that space is abstract, whereas place concerns itself with a "concrete environment invested with emotional value" (Ryan 2015: 87–89). Similarly, interaction design researchers Harrison and Dourish (1996) choose to further differentiate between human concepts of space and place. Space, they suggest, relates to the structure of the world, the three-dimensional environment in which we inhabit. However, in their theory of place, they contrast cultural understandings with those which frame innate human behaviour (Naji et al. 2018: 3).

WHAT IS A MIRROR WORLD, AND WHY DO THEY MATTER?

Ricci et al. (2015) outline that mirror worlds are useful as conceptual models that indicate potential future trends of augmented societies. With the recent resurgence of virtual reality technologies and the relative affordability of devices such as the Microsoft HoloLens and the Oculus as well as the popularity of augmented reality games such as *Pokemon Go* it is easy for us to imagine an augmented future. In fact, as I write this in the year 2020 perhaps it is more accurate to accept that the augmented future is in fact here. Google Maps now offer an augmented reality mode in which the user can switch between AR directions in which directions are superimposed on your live camera view and regular 2D map directions. We are already living in an augmented society as our realities blend with both digital and analogue content daily. Mirroring occurs when objects from the physical analogue world have digital counterparts and vice versa, virtual twins so to speak. This is particularly evident in what are termed now our smart spaces such as digital cities in which algorithms and sensors are equally as influential agents as the human inhabitants (Ricci et al. 2015: 60). A mirror world involves the integration of multiple forms of technology such as mixed reality smart spaces and the Internet of Things. Mirror worlds occur when analogue or physical objects have digital counterparts or digital twins that can be engaged and acted upon by humans as can be found in mixed reality (Ricci et al. 2015: 60–63).

Between Page and Screen

Amaranth Borsuk and Brad Bouse's 2016 *Between Page and Screen* is a useful example of a mixed reality poem to discuss here as Borsuk suggests that mixed reality experiences allow for "an interpenetration of the virtual and physical" (Borsuk 2017: 168). In this example the virtual space becomes reified into our more common analogue place as they use augmented reality technology to make their poetry, resulting in a book containing QR codes which, when combined with a webcam, provides a series of poems that chronicle a love affair between two characters, P and S. The body still matters in virtual spaces and Borsuk (2017: 168) refers to Amanda Starling Gould's body-device ecology in that AR the body is a vector for the poetic content. The body-device concept echoes discussions that have already taken place in this book in Chap. 4, "Haptic Hermeneutics and Poetry Apps," in which I discuss *embodied interaction* (Dourish 2001) in relation to the embodied poetic experience of mobile platform digital poetry. In mobile digital poetry the hand gesture draws the body into the poetic experience, but in VR space the fact that the hand is no longer visible can in fact remove the body from the experience resulting in a disembodied experience. It is however only the illusion of the removal of the body, given the body is very much still there and is required to move through virtual space which, as anyone who has tripped over a chair while in VR will attest, is still very much dependent on the physical space being in existence so that we may interact in the virtual. Although our mirror worlds may seem very real they only exist in relation to the physical, they cannot exist without the physical analogue world whereas the physical world can exist quite easily without the virtual. Equally though we may enter virtual spaces in order to feel what Anderson terms *bodilessness* (Anderson and Huang 2017), this can only be achieved by having a body to leave behind in the first place.

SUMMARY

This chapter examined examples of mixed reality poetry in order to unpack the changing role of words in virtual spaces that can operate as sculptural object but also as affordances for embodied interaction. Consideration was also given to the interpenetration of virtual space into our analogue places as mixed reality poetry forces us to think about our digital twins and mirror worlds as environments that offer as much communicative potential as the printed page, albeit in completely transformed modalities. The interactive poetic experience continues to be embodied through the materialities of bodily gestures in virtual spaces that reflect our analogue worlds and therefore transport our existing frameworks of meanings from our analogue space into digital mirror worlds that distort our relationships to the written word which becomes a dynamic sculptural object.

REFERENCES

Anderson, L., and H-C. Huang. 2017. *Chalkroom*. 74th Venice International Film Festival, Venice, Italy, September 1–9.

Anderson, L., and B. Marranca. 2018. Laurie Anderson: Telling Stories in Virtual Reality. *PAJ: A Journal of Performance and Art* 40 (3): 37–44.

Borsuk, A. 2017. Between Page & Screen. In *#WomenTechLit*, ed. M. Mencia. Morgantown: West Virginia University Press.

Borsuk, A., and B. Bouse. 2016. *Between Page and Screen*. Denver: SpringGun Press.

Breeze, M. 2018. All the Delicate Duplicates: Game Building with[In] Mezangelle. In *TEXT Special Issue 49: Writing and Gaming*, ed. R. Watkins, M. Takolander, A. Cole, and R. Davis, April. Accessed 16 August 2020. http://www.textjournal.com.au/speciss/issue49/Breeze.pdf.

Breeze, M., and A. Campbell. 2017. *All the Delicate Duplicates*, Dreaming Methods. http://dreamingmethods.itch.io.

Cayley, J. 2006. Lens: The Practice and Poetics of Writing in Immersive VR: A Case Study with Maquette. *Leonardo Electronic Almanac* 14 (5–6). Accessed 13 August 2017. http://leoalmanac.org/journal/vol_14/lea_v14_n05-06/jcayley.asp.

Cramer F. 2002. MEZ, 'RE(AD.HTM'. Accessed 7 September 2020. http://cramer.pleintekst.nl/all/mez/mez-presentation.pdf.

Dourish, P. 2001. 'Where The Action Is: The Foundations of Embodied Interaction'. Massachusetts: MIT Press.

Electronic Literature Organisation. n.d.-a. Online. Accessed 7 September 2020. https://eliterature.org/about/120/.

————. n.d.-b. Online. Content by Keyword. *Electronic Literature Collection Volume Two.* Accessed 7 September 2020. https://collection.eliterature. org/2/extra/keywords.html.

Fitzgerald, E. 1993. *The Rubáiyát of Omar Khayyám.* London: Avenel Books.

Funkhouser, C.T. 2012. *New Directions in Digital Poetry.* London: Continuum.

Haraway, D. 1988. Situated Knowledges: The Science Question in Feminism and the Privilege of Partial Perspective. *Feminist Studies* 14 (3): 575–599. Published by: Feminist Studies, Inc. http://www.jstor.org/stable/3178066.

Harrison, S., and Dourish, P. 1996. Re-place-ing space: the roles of place and space in collaborative systems. ACM conference on Computer supported cooperative work. Boston: Harrison S, Dourish P. Re-place-ing space: the roles of place and space in collaborative systems. InProceedings of the 1996 ACM conference on Computer supported cooperative work 1996 Nov 16 (pp. 67–76). ACM.

Kress, G. 2003. *Literacy in the New Media Age.* Oxon and New York: Routledge.

Lashley, M.C., and B. Creech. 2017. Voices for a New Vernacular: A Forum on Digital Storytelling Interview with Janet Murray. *International Journal of Communication (19328036)* 11: 1078–1080, 3p.

Milgram, P., H. Takemura, A. Utsumi, and F. Kishino. 1995. Augmented Reality: A Class of Displays on the Reality-Virtuality Continuum. In *Telemanipulator and Telepresence Technologies,* vol. 2351, 282–293. International Society for Optics and Photonics.

Murray, J. 2017. *Hamlet on the Holodeck, the Future of Narrative in Cyberspace.* Cambridge, MA: The MIT Press.

Naji, J., G. Young, and S. Stehle. 2018. *Places in Virtual Space: An Analysis of Geospatial Data Narratives Presented in Cross-Reality Visualisations.* 58th ERSA Congress, University College Cork, Ireland. https://az659834.vo. msecnd.net/eventsairwesteuprod/production-ersa-public/eb2a5d37e573431 cb13e25e642c4168a.

Naji, J., G. Subramaniam, and G. White. 2019. *New Approaches to Literature for Language Learning.* Switzerland: Palgrave Macmillan.

Nash Cadell, J.E. 1899. *The Rubáiyát of Omar Khayyám.* New York: John Lane.

O'Sullivan, J. 2019. *Towards a Digital Poetics: Electronic Literature & Literary Games.* Accessed 16 August 2020. http://www.amazon.co.uk/kindlestore.

Ricci, A., M. Piunti, L. Tummolini, and C. Castelfranchi. 2015. The Mirror World: Preparing for Mixed-Reality Living. *IEEE Pervasive Computing* 14 (2): 60–63.

Ryan, M.L. 2015. *Narrative as Virtual Reality 2: Revisiting Immersion and Interactivity in Literature and Electronic Media.* Baltimore: JHU Press.

Ryan, M., K. Foote, and M. Azaryahu. 2016. *Narrating Space/Spatializing Narrative: Where Narrative Theory and Geography Meet.* The Ohio State University Press.

Simanowski, R. 2010. Digital Anthropophagy: Refashioning Words as Image, Sound and Action. *Leonardo* 43(2), 159–163. Cambridge, MA: The MIT Press. Accessed 29 August 2018, Project MUSE Database.

Strehovec, J. 2010. Alphabet on the Move. In *Reading Moving Letters: Digital Literature in Research and Teaching. A Handbook*, ed. R. Simanowski, J. Schäfer, and P. Gendolla. London: Transaction Publishers.

———. 2017. Vanishing Letters in Text-based Digital Installations. *First Monday* 22 (2). https://doi.org/10.5210/fm.v22i2.6811.

Wilsher, M. 2019. Virtual and Other Bodies. *Art Monthly*, (427), pp. 11–14. Accessed 16 August 2020. https://search-ebscohost-com.jproxy.nuim.ie/login.aspx?direct=true&db=a9h&AN=136701602&site=ehost-live.

CHAPTER 7

Conclusion: Future Poetics—Literary Expression in the Second Age of Machines

Abstract This chapter provides a short critical overview of digital poetry by synopsising conclusions from previous chapters. Digital poetry is situated within the second age of machines and the resulting implications of this on human thought within the context of literary expression and modern poetic writing are discussed. The resulting loss of interpretative autonomy for the human interpreter is highlighted and a core conclusion is formulated that emphasises the need to factor in the coding of literary algorithms as a kind of poetic writing that reformulates human autonomy into the digital poetry process. Discussions in this chapter take place regarding the future of poetry so that we may begin to understand how the literary experience is transformed in contemporary computing environments.

Keywords Machine writing • Digital poetry • Literary expression • Human thought • Algorithms

A SHORT CRITICAL OVERVIEW OF DIGITAL POETRY

This book began with an introduction in Chap. 1 that identified the digital poetry artefact as a hybridic object that inhabits a dynamic networked landscape of differing techno-environments. The value and topicality of digital poetry research were highlighted, and each chapter of this book was introduced in order to set the groundwork for the following chapters. The broad issues of hermeneutics, posthumanism, gesture as meaning making and technosocial multimodal communication were introduced along with their relevance to the critical analysis of digital poetry.

Chap. 2, "What Is Digital Poetry?" recapped on existing research, practice and publications in the area of digital poetry while situating it within the field of electronic literature. This chapter gave a brief synopsis of the field while outlining how digital poetry identification and categorisation is a seemingly endless task given it is inexorably linked to the development of digital technologies. Digital poems are more usefully identified as processes (as per Hayles 2006: 181), hybridic (as per Funkhouser 2007: 223–234), technocentric (as per Strehovec 2020: Online) and mutable (as per Strehovec 2010: 71; Flores 2013: 108). The defining elements of a digital poem were also discussed in order to conclude *that movement, audio, visuals and interactivity are not always required to be present in order to identify a digital poem, rather instead, and crucially, a digital poem is one that could only have been made using a computer.* Given its technocentric nature, digital poetry has historically been identified by the technologies that have created them meaning that many forms are now defunct. This is why part of the aim of this book was to not only critically analyse examples of digital poetry but also identify, document and discuss some of the newer forms of digital poetry such as *Instapoetry, Mobile Poetry Apps, Drone Poetry, Digital Eco-Poetry and Mixed Reality poetry which encompasses VR and AR poetry.*

Chapter 3, "Instapoetics and the Literary Algorithm," examined the tension between code and language in the semiotic space of digital poetry using Instagram and Machine Learning poetry examples. The hermeneutic potential of the techno-environment in which digital poetry lives was recognised as well as the impact of the social dimensions of algorithmical poetry such as demographics of gender and race. Semiotic modes of interpretation were seen to remain a factor, as they are in traditional print poetry, in the incorporation of visual and aural modes of communication and the interactive potential of the multimodal space.

Up to now theories of multimodality have offered us an expanded approach to meaning making that takes into consideration multiple dimensions of representation such as still and moving images, music, art, voice narration, dubbing, subtitles, word-bubbles and so on (Naji et al. 2019: 150); however, now the move to immersive computing technologies has changed the parameters of multimodality once more. At first glance the reintroduction of spatial and gestural parameters to a multi-modal framework could easily lull us into the belief that we are in fact returning to a more "authentic" communicative process one that harks back to non-mediated human communication minus the olfactory and gustatory modalities. This I would argue is a dangerous position to take as it fails to consider the medium specificity of MR and the particular nego-tiation that takes place between the biological, psychological, affective, social, economic and technological affordances of a range of highly dynamic actors (Jarrett and Naji 2016). Digital poetry inhabits a net-worked environment in which meaning is formed in a dynamic way in relation to other actors within the network. The more I research digital poetry the more complex it becomes and the realisation that *each different type of digital poetry requires different aspects to be considered because of the vastly differing socio-techno environments they inhabit.*

Chapter 4, "Haptic Hermeneutics and Poetry Apps," in particular dealt with the loss of autonomy of the human interpreter. This chapter sought to develop a theory of interpretation or meaning making for digital poetry on mobile platforms by recognising the unique nature of gesture required for interaction with haptic devices. In doing so Capurro (2010: 35) was cited, in order to use a digital hermeneutics framework that recognised the loss of autonomy of the human interpreter in the human conversations mediated by digital technologies which then correspondingly questioned the interpretational autonomy of human agents (Capurro 2010: 36). *This key point builds on a posthuman framework in order to recognise the interpre-tative potential that exists in mobile digital poetry for ALL actors and that interpretation can take place on both the human and machine side of the digital poetry process.*

Chapter 5, "Eco-writing and Drone: Digital Poetry During the Anthropocene," questioned technocentric approaches to digital poetry and has critically questioned the use of digital tools and technologies in examples of digital eco-writing that look to highlight ecological concerns. Notably digital ecopoetry is the only form of digital poetry in this book which takes a less technocentric approach and is not identified or catego-rised by the technologies that created it. Instead like print ecopoetry, it is identified by its themes. Gould's (2016) digital environmental media studies approach was a useful methodology that sought to highlight eco-logical concerns in relation to digital technological practice in a thought-ful manner that could be incorporated into digital literary practice. Brady's (2016) *Drone Poetics* was discussed in terms of how they indicate the need for a revision of our thinking regarding the practice of writing poetry in the drone age.

This book looks at just some examples of contemporary digital poetry that I have come across in my own research and there are many, many, more in existence. The communicative and collaborative capacity of computer technology transformed literature from the page to the screen, now through poetry in the second machine age we can see that we are witnessing another transformation as we move away from the screen to virtual environments. Chapter 6, "Poetic Mirror Worlds and Mixed Reality Poetry," focused on this transition to virtual environments by examining examples of mixed reality poetry in order to unpack the changing role of words in virtual spaces that can operate as sculptural objects but also as affordances for embodied interaction. Consideration was also given to the interpenetration of virtual space into our analogue places as mixed reality poetry forces us to think about our digital twins and mirror worlds as environments that offer as much communicative potential as the printed page, albeit in completely transformed modalities. The interactive poetic experience continues to be embodied through the materialities of bodily gestures in virtual spaces that reflect our analogue worlds and therefore transport our existing frameworks of meanings from our analogue space into digital mirror worlds that distort our relationships to the written word which becomes a dynamic sculptural object.

Modern Poetic Writing

No matter the differing socio-techno environments, discussions to date have shown that some elements of digital poetry are similar and because of this warrant closer examination; *the core commonality in all digital poetry processes would appear to be the algorithm and the human interpreter.* At the interpretation end of the digital poetry process the advent of machine learning has meant that the algorithm has gained agency and the human interpreter has lost some, certainly when it comes to "reading" the final poetic output. Most machine learning literary examples rely on the machine first "reading" existing literary texts. However human agency and autonomy can still be seen to be paramount at the creation point of a digital poem if we consider the writing of the algorithm to be part of the literary process. Therefore, the future of digital poetry needs to account for modern poetic writing incorporating the coding of algorithms with literary functions as well as final poetic text outputs. The definition of a literary algorithm therefore needs to be relational, as function, intention and interpretation have to be considered. The function of a literary algorithm and whether the human interpreter intended or interpreted a literary meaning from the process can define a literary algorithm. If the function of the code is to make a poem it can be considered a literary algorithm, or if the function of the code is not obviously literary but the intention of the human author was to create a literary object then it can be deemed a literary algorithm. Alternatively, if the human interpreter constructs literary meaning from the digital object even if the function and human author did not intend it then it too can be deemed a literary algorithm. As Chap. 3, "Instapoetics and the Literary Algorithm," concluded *a literary algorithm can be defined in relation to the intention of the human interpreter and author engaged in the digital poetry process.*

Machine Autonomy

As I sit at my desk writing this book, the window is open, and it is a sunny pleasant day. Outside I can hear human voices, children playing, adults conversing, animal noises too, of dogs and birds, but also most noticeably for the purposes of this book I can hear the loud thumps, whirrs and bangs of machines everywhere. Perhaps if I had chosen engineering as my undergraduate degree instead of writing I may be able to identify the functions of each of these machines just from their various sounds, which I didn't and I can't, but I do note that they are as active outside as the human participants. We share our world with machines, and this began quite some time ago with the first age of machines which spanned the early to mid-twentieth century and refers to an era of humanity in which our progress was driven primarily by technological innovation brought about by the industrial revolution. Humans were no longer reliant on human or animal labour, instead we could, for example, harvest and transport large quantities of produce with tractors and trains (Brynjolfsson and McAfee 2014: 6–7). Now we are in the second machine age, when we no longer have to rely on human brain power and instead, we are using computers to calculate, think, remember (Brynjolfsson and McAfee 2014: 7–8) and most notably write literary texts. Hauer (2018: 106) gives the example of programmer Zack Thoutt's decision to finish George R. R. Martin's *A Song of Ice and Fire*, fans had long despaired of waiting for the final instalment to be written. Zack therefore decided to get an artificial neural network to read what had been written so far and then write the ending. There goes our autonomy.

This leads us to one of the most striking conclusions arrived at during the course of this book, specifically thanks to Capurro's (2010: 36) digital hermeneutics, which is *the recognition of the loss of autonomy of the human interpreter in the digital literary process*. The post-human position of a dynamic process at play that affords agency not only to the human but to the machine and the algorithms, thereby accounting for vast variations of interpretation depending on different platforms and devices, is no longer a ground-breaking conclusion and is one that is particularly well established, in digital media circles at least. What isn't well established however is the fact that, thanks to machine learning, *digital poetic interpretation now takes place not only on the human side but on the machine side too, and as a result the human side has experienced a loss of autonomy.*

Machine Transformation of Thought

The synopsis of this book's chapters' conclusions above identifies digital poetry as a unique hybridic techno-social literary artifact that reflects the changing, dare I say evolving, nature of human thought and communication. Rettberg (2019: 18) asserts that electronic literature texts "present us with crafted experiences that reflect changes wrought by the digital turn taking place in the nature of communication, textuality, society, and perhaps even the structure of human thought." Rettberg is referring to the wider field of electronic literature of which digital poetry makes up a component, a core component I would argue that distils the core nature of literary expression and interpretation.

The communicative and collaborative capacity of computer technology transformed literature from the page to the screen, now through contemporary technological developments we can see that we are witnessing another transformation as we move away from the screen to virtual environments and autonomous algorithms. What happens to the poetic form in this virtual space? What happens to human expression when we recognise the loss of autonomy of the human interpreter? What happens to text? Reading? Writing? Can we even use these terms so associated with print anymore? This book has sought to answer these pressing and vital questions so that we may begin to understand the true impact of the second age of machines that we are only just beginning to enter. We commonly refer to "the language of film," or "the language of art," and now we are referring to the language of machines. This transformation of thought enabled by digital technologies obviously has wide reaching implications. This book has sought to focus on a small "cyberspec" of it by using digital poetry as a unique literary artefact that might serve as a case study of sorts with which we can analyse changing human subjectivities in the second age of machines.

Summary

This chapter synopsised this book's forward facing critical technocentric approach to digital poetry as a mutable and hybridic artefact that is emblematic of human subjectivities in cyberspace. Contemporary digital poetry techno-environments from mobile platforms, such as Instagram, to mixed reality and remotely piloted aircraft have been discussed in order to chart the constantly changing shape of the digital poem. This conclusion chapter framed digital poetry in the second age of machines in which human autonomy is diminished and poetic writing can be found within the functions of algorithms.

References

Brady, A. 2016. Drone Poetics. *New Formations* 89: 116–136.

Brynjolfsson, E., and A. McAfee. 2014. *The Second Machine Age : Work, Progress, and Prosperity in a Time of Brilliant Technologies*. 1st ed. New York: W.W. Norton & Company.

Capurro, R. 2010. Digital Hermeneutics: An Outline. *AI & Soc* 25: 35–42. https://doi.org/10.1007/s00146-009-0255-9.

Flores, L. 2013. Digital Textuality and Its Behaviors. *Journal of Comparative Literature and Aesthetics* 36 (1–2): 97+. *Gale Academic OneFile*. Accessed 2 October 2020. https://link.gale.com/apps/doc/A411197582/AONE?u=nu im&sid=AONE&xid=49a40964.

Funkhouser, C.T. 2007. *Prehistoric Digital Poetry: An Archaeology of Forms, 1959–1995. Alabama: The.* University of Alabama Press.

Gould, A. 2016. Restor(y)ing the Ground: Digital Environmental Media Studies. *Networking Knowledge: Journal of the MeCCSA Postgraduate Network* 9 (5): 1–19.

Hauer, T. 2018. Society and the Second Age of Machines: Algorithms Versus Ethics. *Soc* 55: 100–106. https://doi.org/10.1007/s12115-018-0221-6.

Hayles, N.K. 2006. The Time of Digital Poetry: From Object to Event. In *New Media Poetics: Contexts, Technotexts, and Theories*, ed. A. Morris and T. Swiss. Cambridge, MA: The MIT Press.

Jarrett, K., and J. Naji. 2016. What Would Media Studies Do? Social Media Shakespeare as a Technosocial Process. In *Borrowers and Lenders: The Journal of Shakespeare and Appropriation*. http://www.borrowers.uga.edu/1794/show.

Naji, J., G. Subramaniam, and G. White. 2019. *New Approaches to Literature for Language Learning*. Switzerland: Palgrave Macmillan.

Rettberg, S. 2019. *Electronic Literature*. Cambridge: Polity.

Strehovec, J. 2010. Alphabet on the Move. In *Reading Moving Letters: Digital Literature in Research and Teaching. A Handbook*, ed. R. Simanowski, J. Schäfer, and P. Gendolla. London: Transaction Publishers.

———. 2020. Smart Technology Instead of Blood and Soil. *Electronic Book Review*, 5 July. Accessed 15 September 2020. https://doi.org/10.7273/3rjs-cl10.

Author Index[1]

[1] Note: Page numbers followed by 'n' refer to notes.

Subject Index[1]

[1] Note: Page numbers followed by 'n' refer to notes.

CPSIA information can be obtained
at www.ICGtesting.com
Printed in the USA
BVHW041302080321
602003BV00005B/62